Interwoven in Jerry Sutton's new ~~theology~~, good history, and good hermeneutics. One ~~finds~~ in this primer on biblical preaching a very important thread of great practicality. Sutton's book does provide a clear method of how to design, develop, and deliver biblical sermons. In this book, you will learn how to connect with the great preachers of history, biblical imperatives about communicating the gospel, and how to connect with people where they are. His masterful grasp of a multitude of disciplines shows forth in this work on preaching. This text comes at a needed time where many are struggling to find how to communicate the inerrant Word of God in a twenty-first-century culture that seems to have lost its way. I recommend to you Jerry Sutton's new book

Frank S. Page
President and Chief Executive Officer SBC
Executive Committee Nashville, TN

When I moved to Nashville in 1990 to attend college, I can say that I really did love Jesus. But I didn't truly know how to love Him through His Word. It was under the pastoring of Dr. Jerry Sutton (whom I affectionately knew as Brother Jerry) where learning and growing in the Word became the passion of my life. His strong presence and forthright teaching changed me as a believer. Furthermore, Brother Jerry gave me my first opportunity to be a worship pastor at a church. I'm forever grateful for his Holy Spirit–driven influence in my life through many crucial years. I pray that pastors everywhere will be encouraged, motivated, and sent out by the wisdom God has given this man, just as I have been encouraged, motivated, and sent out.

Travis Cottrell
Worship Leader, Living Proof Live
with Beth Moore, and Worship Pastor,
Englewood Baptist Church, Jackson, TN

As a senior pastor of almost thirty years, I appreciate books on preaching that are penned by veteran pastors. My "heroes" in preaching are men such as Charles Spurgeon, W. A. Criswell, Herschel Hobbs, Jerry Vines, and of course, my predecessor at Bellevue, Adrian Rogers. These men served as busy pastors. They led great churches, shepherded their flocks, and evangelized the lost, while at the same time developed and delivered biblical sermons week in and week out. That is a daunting task indeed!

Jerry Sutton is now a professor of preaching, but for many years he too served as a senior pastor. In his new book, *A Primer on Biblical Preaching*, Dr. Sutton sets forth both professional and practical advice to any preacher who wants to sharpen himself as a proclaimer of God's Word. This work is both comprehensive and compelling. I've known the author for over thirty years. He is a godly man, a family man, a local-church man, and a preaching man. If you want to learn about preaching from a scholar who is also a veteran pastor and practitioner, this book is for you!

Steve Gaines
Senior Pastor, Bellevue Baptist Church,
Memphis, TN

Every pastor knows that his greatest challenge is to preach consistently solid biblical messages. In Jerry Sutton's new book, *A Primer on Biblical Preaching*, he helps equip pastors and preachers do just that. From a wealth of experience, he teaches the "know how" of sermon planning and preparation. Perhaps even more important, he provides a methodology on how to get it done on a weekly as well as a yearly basis. This book provides much-needed assistance in the field of preaching.

Calvin Wittman
Senior Pastor, Applewood Baptist Church,
Wheat Ridge, CO

With this primer, Jerry Sutton offers an insightful view of what it means to preach biblically. It will serve as a great help to those who wish to keep the biblical text primary to their ministry.

Ed Stetzer
President of LifeWay Research, Nashville, TN

In almost every arena of life, the need to communicate effectively is an absolute necessity. For anyone who desires to improve the ability to communicate, I recommend Jerry Sutton's *A Primer on Biblical Preaching*. Yes, it is for preachers. But it can also help each of us who communicates for a living. Dr. Sutton knows how to communicate, and he knows how to help others communicate better. I recommend it highly.

Jay Sekulow
Chief Counsel for the American Center for
Law and Justice, Washington DC

Every preacher of God's Word will greatly benefit from reading Jerry Sutton's *A Primer on Biblical Preaching*. With remarkable clarity, Sutton emphasizes the importance of ensuring faithfulness to the text while at the same time conveying fresh and incisive application to life. Sutton is no novice at preaching, and the reader will be challenged by his grasp of the subject. With an effectiveness sometimes missed in other books on preaching, Sutton drills home the fact that biblical preaching requires a holy life in order to properly handle the holy Word; preaching is meant to change the preacher most of all. Sutton's book belongs in every serious preacher's library.

Tom Elliff
President International Mission Board, SBC

Jerry Sutton brings the experience of a preacher, pastor, and professor to his writing concerning biblical preaching. This manual gets to the nuts and bolts of preaching the Bible. It is pointed and practical. Any gospel preacher would benefit from spending time in this book.

Ted Traylor
Pastor-Olive Baptist Church, Pensacola, FL

As a young seminarian, my wife and I joined the Wedgwood Baptist Church, whose pastor was the author of this work. Some of the most helpful, practical, and real counsel I ever received came from Jerry Sutton. He encouraged me in a way that changed the trajectory of my life, and I am still reaping the benefits of his wisdom. Now he has produced this outstanding work to help many more as he helped me. Read this, preacher. Gain wisdom, gain insight, and gain effectiveness. Most of all, as he describes so well in his second chapter, learn from this man how to be a man of God.

Alvin L. Reid
Professor of Evangelism and Student
Ministry, Bailey Smith Chair of
Evangelism, Southeastern Baptist
Theological Seminary, Wake Forest, NC

Dr. Jerry Sutton's new book on preaching is theological, philosophical, and practical all at the same time. I can think of no other book that contains such a holistic and approachable plan for excellence in biblical preaching.

Evangelicals are people of the Word. Those who are called to preach must do so as if eternity depends upon it ... and it does. Every person who preaches should have a copy of this book in his or her library and revisit it often.

Ben Stroup,
Writer, consultant, and blogger, author of
Church Giving Matters, Nashville, TN

Jerry Sutton has done it again. A superb author, he has prepared one of the most practical volumes on preaching to come along in a long time. He focuses on the message and the messenger, the preparation and the delivery, and the requirements and passion for preaching the Word of God. Every preacher will benefit from these significant pages. Read them with profit to yourself and to those to whom you preach.

Jimmy Draper
President Emeritus, LifeWay Christian
Resources, Fort Worth, TX

When I dialogue with others about preaching and desiring them to be more equipped in the discipline, I want it not just from a scholar but from an experienced pastor. This is why I think Dr. Jerry Sutton's newest book, *A Primer on Biblical Preaching*, is essential to share with others. His years of shepherding God's people through the ups and downs of life and church, coupled with his well-known commitment to scholarship, qualifies him uniquely to produce for us such an outstanding volume as this. This book should be read by those of us who have been in the ministry journey for years but is also a must read for any student of preaching today. Get it, read it, and invest into the lives of other preachers by sharing it with them.

Ronnie W. Floyd
Senior Pastor, Cross Church Springdale AR

The preparation of preachers is a challenge in any age, and Jerry Sutton's book *A Primer on Biblical Preaching* is a solid and helpful contribution to that task. Sutton draws on years of experience as an effective preacher and pastor as he walks readers through the process of developing sermons that are biblically faithful and will connect with listeners. While young preachers will find the book to be a useful starting point for their efforts, veteran preachers will also find much of value as a reminder of the immense challenge and great urgency of the preaching task in the twenty-first century. This volume deserves a place on any preacher's shelf.

Michael Duduit,
Executive Editor, Preaching magazine, and
Dean of the College of Christian Studies,
Anderson University, Anderson, SC

At Liberty University, we have a vision to "build champions for Christ." We do this by attempting to equip each student to become the best informed and best skilled in their field. One way we achieve this goal is by hiring the best authorities possible to train our students.

I am grateful that we had Dr. Jerry Sutton teaching homiletics, a discipline he has practiced effectively for over three decades. I endorse wholeheartedly his new volume, *A Primer on Biblical Preaching*. Every preacher will benefit from studying this insightful volume. Anyone who wants to improve his or her ability to communicate will find assistance.

Elmer Towns
Co-Founder, Liberty University Dean,
Liberty Baptist Theological Seminary and
Graduate School, Lynchburg, VA

In this day and age of white noise that seems to drown out messages of value and life, my longtime friend Dr. Jerry Sutton and his exciting new book, *A Primer on Biblical Preaching*, enables us to lift up our voices like a trumpet. The apostle Paul warned that if the trumpet gives an uncertain sound, how will we ever prepare for battle? With the research of a scholar, the insights of a historian, and the instinct of one of the most accomplished preachers in the land, we are reminded of our privilege and responsibility in doing the heavy lifting of communicating God's Word to this, our generation. This is a practical, motivational, and challenging resource. Pick up this book, absorb it, and then pick up the trumpet, and together may we play reveille instead of taps for our planet and this generation.

Dr. Jay Strack
President, www.studentleadership.net
Editor of the Impact Student Leadership
Bible

I began preaching when I was seventeen years old. In the last thirty-two years, I have read numerous books on preaching, often with sense of loss when it came to the connection of preaching to the larger scheme of ministry, history, and life. Dr. Jerry Sutton has remedied this dilemma in his latest book. In a day where many books are mass produced like a car on an assembly line, it is easy to tell that this book is a labor of love written from the heart of a caring pastor with the burning desire to influence future preachers. While some books on preaching read more like a chemistry lecture espousing formulas for success, rest assured that is not the case with this book. I especially appreciate the admission from Dr. Sutton in chapter seven that way too many preachers allow themselves to become disconnected from their audience. His response is classic: "Some preachers love to preach; others love the people to whom they preach. I want to encourage my students to be the latter." Well said! This is a great book … get it!

David Wheeler
Professor of Evangelism and Student
Ministries, Liberty University, Lynchburg, VA

Who better to write a book on biblical preaching than one individual who is a seasoned practitioner, a biblical scholar, a pastor, a churchman, and a professor? Jerry Sutton, in *A Primer on Biblical Preaching*, makes a significant contribution to what is already a crowded field just by virtue of the remarkable combination of his own life. The serious preacher will be profoundly edified by this volume.

Paige Patterson
President, Southwestern Baptist Theological
Seminary, Fort Worth, Texas

A Primer on Biblical Preaching

Jerry Sutton

CROSSBOOKS
PUBLISHING

CrossBooks™
A Division of LifeWay
1663 Liberty Drive
Bloomington, IN 47403
www.crossbooks.com
Phone: 1-866-879-0502

First published by CrossBooks 6/10/2011

ISBN: 978-1-6150-7819-6 (sc)
ISBN: 978-1-6150-7820-2 (dj)

Library of Congress Control Number: 2011926495

Printed in the United States of America

Dedicated to

Fred Wolfe, who first gave me a love for biblical preaching.

Contents

Acknowledgments

No endeavor like this is a work of one person. Thank-yous are in order.

I want to thank my daughter, Hilary (a freelance journalist), for painstakingly typing and editing the manuscript. I would also like to thank my other daughter, Ashli (an attorney and professor), for offering numerous editorial suggestions.

My appreciation goes out to my graduate assistants over the past two years here at Liberty University—Josh Saefkow, Brad Milks, and Josh Staats—who helped me immensely.

Special thanks go to Robert Matz, who has assisted me in teaching my preaching classes here at Liberty. He has been an invaluable asset in completing this project.

Thanks, too, to Don Hicks and Dave Hirschman, two of my colleagues here at Liberty, for their constant encouragement.

I also wish to express my appreciation to Dave Nemitz and Melissa Tucker, who helped make this writing project a necessity.

Thanks also go out to the deans under whom I have served: Ergun Caner, Dan Mitchell, and Elmer Towns.

I also want to express my profound love and appreciation to my wife, Fern, for her great patience in my writing projects. They always take longer than originally planned.

I also wish to thank my students, who challenge me everyday to be a molder of champions for Christ. I look forward with great anticipation to see how the Lord will use them in the days and years to come.

Finally, I thank the Lord Jesus for calling me into the ministry of preaching and now the ministry of equipping others to preach.

Lynchburg
November 2010

Foreword

It is an honor for me to recommend Dr. Jerry Sutton's new book, *A Primer on Biblical Preaching*. It is a solid, balanced, systematic introduction to the preacher's most important task in the church today. In this book, Dr. Sutton provides a clear method of how to design, develop, and deliver a biblical sermon. He writes from the perspective of a professor in the classroom who has spent over thirty years practicing what he now teaches for us here at Liberty Baptist Theological Seminary. He knows his discipline.

Jerry has a passion for knowing Christ and his true desire is to help others know Him as well. He knows the Bible and wants to help others grab hold of the wonderful truths and promises found within its pages. His approach to preaching is to assist his listeners in obtaining a strategic understanding of the Bible and bring their lives into conformity to its teaching.

He also knows the church and has a great desire to help churches be healthy through the proclamation of the Word. As a pastor for over thirty years, he has an outstanding track record of being an effective Bible preacher. And, he has proven that he knows what it takes for churches to thrive and grow.

He knows history and can help teach his readers from the wealth of great preachers from bygone eras. Because of his proficiency in history, he can cut through some of the hype which surrounds much of today's approaches to preaching. Jerry will also not be bluffed into embracing generalizations that do not square with great historical preachers and their preaching.

He knows discipleship and equipping. For years he has mentored young preachers who now minister around the world. He understands what it takes to equip the next generation of great preachers because he has done it himself and is continuing to come alongside the preachers of tomorrow.

He knows pastors because he has been one over the long haul. He knows their burdens, stresses, challenges, and struggles. He knows what it is like to have more to do than time permits. He knows what it means to lead and serve in times of great blessing as well as in times of great adversity.

He also knows preaching and what it is like to preach to the same congregation over an extended period of time. He is teaching what he has done. And, he has done it well.

This book should be a must-read for three groups: first, for those who want to learn how to preach; second, for those who need a refresher course on the discipline of preaching; and third, for those who want to know what their pastor must do to be effective in the pulpit. In short, it can help anyone who wants to be a more effective communicator.

Dr. Sutton was a friend of my father and has preached many times in the pulpit at Thomas Road. He is also my friend. I recommend his latest book, *A Primer on Biblical Preaching* without reservation for anyone who needs concrete help in preaching the unchanging Word of God. Dr. Sutton is a pro and he can help you get it done!

Jonathan Falwell

Preface

Like the myriad of men who call themselves "preacher," it has been my calling in life for over a third of a century to stand most weeks before a congregation and share a message from God's Word with a people that I love. Nothing is more important or more vital than for the Word of God to be proclaimed clearly and passionately to a listening world. I am convinced that the unfolding of history is dependent upon what the church does with what it hears. It is for the preparation of the next generation of preachers and the encouragement of the present generation of preachers that I offer this volume.

I have entitled this volume *A Primer on Biblical Preaching.* Consider the title. A primer is a book that covers the basic elements of a subject. It is a textbook giving the first principles of a discipline. This text is not exhaustive. It is a compilation of the essential elements for biblical preaching. It is intended to serve as an introduction to the discipline.

The second part of the title is the word *biblical.* My intention is to help the student become the best communicator of biblical truth possible. My assumption is that God has revealed Himself to humanity and that part of His revelation is Scripture. The task of the preacher is to understand what it says, determine what it means, communicate its implications, and call for a response.

The third part of my title is *preaching.* Definitions of preaching are legion. Here is mine:

Biblical Preaching is the event of verbally communicating a message which is rooted in Scripture by a spokesman representing God to either believers (for the purpose of communicating His truth, reproof, correction, or instruction), or to unbelievers (with a view to their conversion or judgment) with the ultimate intention of bringing all hearers into Christian maturity and the culture into Christian conformity.

My purpose is to equip those called to preach with the necessary skills and tools to fully carry out their calling.

The discipline of preaching is over three thousand years old. Christianity (and before it, Judaism) is essentially a religion of the Word of God.

In John Stott's assessment, "We must speak what He has spoken. Hence the paramount obligation to preach."[1]

When Paul wrote his second epistle to Timothy, he gave his student a solemn charge to preach the Word (2 Tim. 4:1–2). That same charge has been given to every Christian preacher from that day forward. My desire is to help students fulfill that calling in this generation.

An extraordinary set of circumstances brought me here to Liberty in 2009 after serving as a senior pastor for over three decades and preaching thousands of sermons; I now have the opportunity to teach hundreds of students the skills and disciplines that I have cultivated over the years. In this volume, I want to share with you, in a simple format, the process necessary to design, develop, and deliver biblical messages.

I am grateful to the men who taught me and modeled for me the discipline of biblical preaching. When I attended seminary, our textbook for preaching was *Steps to the Sermon*. It was a simple, straightforward approach to preaching biblical messages. My desire is that this volume would serve in our day what that text did for me in my formative years. The first book I read in seminary was Martyn Lloyd-Jones's *Preaching and Preachers*. More than anything else, it taught me that I must be something before I could do something. Preaching is, first and foremost, living the life of Christ and *then* sharing the life of Christ. In biblical terms, the indicative precedes the imperative. First be; then do.

I choose to follow Haddon Robinson's terminology of "biblical preaching" rather than the more popular term "expository preaching." Although I believe that the majority of messages should encompass the exposition of a singular text, I cannot justify biblically or historically the notion that only expository preaching in its narrow definition is authentic preaching. Al Mohler states in his *He Is Not Silent,* "I believe that the only form of authentic Christian preaching is expository preaching." If that absolutely is the case, then Jonathan Edwards's classic, "Sinners in the Hands of an Angry God" is not authentic Christian preaching

---

1   John R. W. Stott, *Between Two Worlds: The Art of Preaching in the Twentieth Century* (Grand Rapids: Wm. B. Eerdmans, 1982), 15.

because, strictly speaking, it is not an exposition of his text, although none would dispute that it is a biblical message. Neither would W. A. Criswell's "Whether We Live or Die" make the cut. In short, I prefer the term biblical preaching and I defer to John Stott's broader definition of expository preaching.[2]

I offer this text to my students as a simple introduction to the disciplines of biblical preaching. I anticipate following this with a multi-volume set of works on the various areas addressed in the book.

In my homiletics classes, I tell my students that Christ can return at any moment, so live with a sense of expectancy. Nonetheless, should He "tarry," as the old preachers used to say, I want my students to be prepared for a ministry that could last fifty or even seventy-five years. To do this, I spend a great deal of time attempting to give them a set of tools which they can use for a lifetime of ministry. In fact, I tell them that it is my desire for them when they have completed my classes that the notes they have and the skills we have worked on will constitute a tool box to which they can return as needed. This book is that toolbox, and my hope is that you will find it helpful as you seek to gain the skills necessary to become an effective biblical preacher. Understand, please, that in many places I will revert to the second person plural *you* as I seek not just to be casual, but personal, as if I were having a one-on-one conversation with a student.

Jerry Sutton
Lynchburg, Virginia
September 2010

---

2   R. Albert Mohler, Jr., *He Is Not Silent* (Chicago: Moody Press, 2008), 49.

Chapter 1

An Introduction to Biblical Preaching

Over the years, I've been blessed to travel all over the world. When I travel, I want to follow an itinerary. If I am driving, I want a roadmap. I want to know how I am getting from the point of departure to my final destination. That is the way I am wired, and that is the way I teach. I want a roadmap.

Consider this chapter a roadmap for the study of preaching. John Broadus called his seminal work, *On the Preparation and Delivery of Sermons*. And in a concise statement, that too is the subject matter of this text. My goal is to equip you to be an effective biblical preacher. Consider each chapter a tool in your toolbox. Each chapter is a vital step on your journey to becoming an effective communicator of God's Word.

As mentioned earlier, foundational to becoming an effective preacher is the simple fact that you must be called to preach. You must *be* something (called) before you can *do* something (preach). Your calling is the coming together of several factors. First, God calls those who are saved. Understanding that several pivotal biblical figures, Jeremiah, John the Baptist, and Paul, for example, were called from their mothers' wombs does not negate the fact that normally, only the saved are called. Second, understand that God equips those He calls. Coupled with this is the subjective role of the Holy Spirit, who impresses upon the preacher a sense that this is uniquely the will of God.

Growing up, I had an unfolding awareness that being a preacher might be God's will for my life. In college, I was assigned an Edmund S. Morgan book, *The Puritan Dilemma,* to read for a history class. This volume, a

1

biography of John Winthrop, contained excerpts from his journal. As he deliberated about coming to America, Winthrop penned these words: "When God intends a man to a work he sets a bias in his heart so as though he be tumbled this way and that yet his bias still draws him to that side, and there he rests at last."[3] This experience is replicated in the heart of every God-called preacher.

So here is a brief checklist. First, are you saved? Second, do you display any giftedness necessary for a preaching ministry? And third, is there an inner conviction that you must preach? If the answer to each of these is yes, then you can be reasonably sure that you have the call of God upon your life. A fourth component that normally accompanies these three is the external witness of the church. Those who know you validate in their assessment that you are called to preach.

As we make our way through the process of preparing to preach biblical messages, understand that it starts with the God-called preacher. In chapter two, I want to address the idea of the preacher being a man of God. Particularly, I want to focus on the role of the pastor-teacher (see Eph. 4:11). I know many in the church have speaking/communication responsibilities. Student ministers preach to students. Women's ministers speak to the ladies of the church. Evangelists are invited for special services. Yet, by and large, the preaching ministry rests in the hands of the pastor of the local congregation.

In this chapter, I will address several key issues. First, I want to review the terms used in the New Testament to describe the pastor and his ministry in the local church. For example, Acts 1:8 tells us that we are witnesses. Acts 20:17 identifies leaders of the local congregation as elders. We will review these in order to provide both an overview and a context for the preaching ministry.

In this chapter, I will also provide some practical advice for the God-called preacher. It is the kind of advice that I wish I had received early in my ministry.

The last portion of this chapter will focus on what it means to be a "man of God." I will address his identity from 2 Timothy 6:11–14, his journey from 2 Timothy 3:14–4:2, and his equipping from Luke 2:52. I will conclude, again, with some specific suggestions.

Chapter three will provide a simple overview of the role of hermeneutics in preaching. Hermeneutics, simply put, is the art and science of interpretation. I will introduce this chapter with a set of guidelines that

---

3   Edmund S. Morgan, *The Puritan Dilemma* (Boston: Little, Brown, 1958), 38.

will, hopefully, assist students to develop sound skills in their work of biblical interpretations. Next, we will examine the general principles each student must grasp in order to interpret Scripture accurately. These will be followed by reviewing more particular principles.

After reviewing these overarching principles, we will examine a process that is conducive to helping students deal with a particular passage of Scripture. In short, students will learn to ask the right questions. I like the simple progression of, "What?" "So what?" and "Now what?" In a more expanded format, we ask, what does the text say exactly? What does this text mean? Then, what am I supposed to do with what this text says and means? Vines and Shaddix identify this as an investigation, interpretation, and implication. And this, too, is a sound approach to understanding how best to interpret the text before us.

After reviewing the major concepts in the study of hermeneutics, chapter four will turn to the subject: what is biblical preaching? We will begin by reviewing the principal words for preaching in the New Testament. Next, we will examine some definitions by various scholars and preachers of the preaching task, and finally, we will examine my working definition of biblical preaching.

> Biblical preaching is the event of verbally communicating a message that is rooted in Scripture by a spokesman representing God to either believers (for the purpose of communicating His truth, reproof, correction, or instruction), or to unbelievers (with a view to their conversion or judgment) with the ultimate intention of bringing all hearers into Christian maturity and the culture into Christian conformity.

In this chapter, I will break down my working definition into its component parts. My goal is to help students clarify just exactly what it is they have been called to do.

Chapter five will give suggestions on sources of sermon ideas. It will also provide a step-by-step plan to help you plan your preaching for a calendar year. My professors called this a Planned Program of Preaching. I have mine going back almost thirty years. In this chapter, we will also consider some insights on selecting titles and texts.

Chapter six will provide a succinct overview of the history of preaching. In order to understand the significance of preaching today, it is of critical importance to understand how preaching has developed since the time of Christ's incarnation. This chapter will begin, however, with biblical preaching touching on the preaching of Moses, the prophets, the Gospels, and Acts. Following the New Testament era is the Patristic period. The early church fathers, the Apologists, and even the heretics all teach us about preaching. We will give special attention to the preaching of Chrysostom, Ambrose, and Augustine.

Preaching in the medieval church spans over a thousand years. Here, we will examine the preaching during the dark ages and the Scholastic period. Attention will be given to the work of Bernard of Clairvaux, Dominic, and Francis. In the pre-Reformation era, the work of Huss, Wycliff, and Savonarola will be examined.

A review of the preaching during the Reformation era will begin with the work of Erasmus, although I consider him the last of the pre-Reformers. Most students of preaching are unaware that his last work, *Ecclesiastes,* is a treatise on preaching.

After providing some general observations of Reformation preaching, attention will be given to the preaching of Luther, Zwingli, Hubmaier, Calvin, Arminius, Latimer, and Knox.

Following the Reformation age, we will examine the preaching of the Puritans and the Pietists. Baxter, Bunyan, and Spener will be highlighted.

From here, we will move into a study of the preaching in the First Great Awakening, which was known as the Evangelical Awakening in Europe. We will review the preaching of Wesley, Whitefield, and Edwards. Next, we will give attention to the preaching of the Second Great Awakening and the work of Timothy Dwight.

As we move into the nineteenth century, the preaching of Finney and Moody will be noted. Then, we will examine the preaching of Spurgeon, who is known as the "Prince of Preachers." We will conclude with preaching in the twentieth and twenty-first centuries and provide some general observations of what we have learned.

Chapter seven will address issues related to connecting with those who listen. The old adage is true: "People don't care how much you know until they know how much you care." Some preachers love to preach; others love the people to whom they preach. I want to encourage my students to be the latter.

Whenever I speak, I always begin by asking three questions: Who am I speaking to? What are their needs? And what does God say?

If we are going to connect with our listeners, we have to know what is in their concern zone. Where are they hurting? Where are they hungry? What are their interests? When Jesus preached, He always started where the people were. Why should we approach the preaching task any differently?

We also need to ask the question, "What kind of listener am I dealing with?" Different people are wired differently. Study the people you preach to in order to learn how best to connect with them.

When it comes to connecting with people, we need to learn how to ask the right questions. As we build our message, I believe it is important to consider what is the most practical, positive, encouraging, simple, personal, interesting, and creative way to say what needs to be said. Some of the questions come from Rick Warren's lecture, "How to Communicate to Change Lives." I recommend it.

Chapter eight details the ingredients of a great sermon. Just like a great meal requires great ingredients, or a custom-built house requires superior building materials, a great sermon requires great ingredients. So, what are those ingredients? It starts with the need for a credible spokesman. This addresses issues of character, integrity, competence, transparency, authority, and humility. Second, it must have a clear biblical message. It must be driven by, anchored in, and surface from the text.

Third, it connects the truth of Scripture with where people live. Next, it uses clear and vivid illustrations. These must be accurate, descriptive, appropriate, and timely. Fifth, it must be practically applied. In short, the listener must know exactly what demands are made by the Word of God.

The next ingredient is the quality of a logical flow. Does each point connect to the whole? Can one hearing the message discern that all the parts connect? Does it lead up to a logical climax? Coupled with this is the observation that this message must be balanced. Appropriate attention is given to explanation, illustration, argumentation, and application.

Next, it is relevant. Those who hear know exactly what the Word of God demands. They know how it affects what they believe, feel, and do (or need to quit doing). Coupled with relevant is the quality of timeliness. This too is part of the ingredient of relevance.

The next ingredient is that it must be well delivered. Among other things, the preacher should make eye contact, use full vocal production, make appropriate gestures, use dramatic pauses, and keep distracting mannerisms to a minimum.

I believe that the next ingredient is that the preacher should preach for a verdict. Preachers must impress upon their listeners that God demands a decision.

The final ingredient is that the message must be anointed by the Holy Spirit. This will not happen without prayer, purity, and preparation.

Chapter nine will detail the process of sermon preparation. If the ingredients are assembled, the question remains as to how to put it all together. How do I prepare this spiritual meal? How do I build this spiritual home? Here, we focus on the word *process*. Process, like time, is the unfolding of a sequence of events. So how can you ensure that you are doing the best job of facilitating the process? In this chapter, I will give you a methodology I have used. What I tell my students here at Liberty is that I will teach you a method and a process and you are free to alter it to fit your own style. I have many friends who are senior pastors, and no two of them follow exactly the same method. So, establish a method that works for you and stay with it.

Preparing a sermon is like building a house. It is a process that follows a sequential pattern. I will teach you this method and then tell you to feel free to adapt it to your time schedule, personality, and priorities.

Chapter ten focuses on the exposition of the text. After selecting the text from which you will preach, five preliminary questions come first. What is the genre? What is the context, and what specifically does this text say? As we dig deeper, we ask, what does this text mean? Then, what are its essential truths?

Again, here are several keys as you work on your exposition. Study the text until you know what it says. Study your text until you know what it means. Use Scripture to interpret Scripture. View your text with respect to "progressive revelation." Finally, always view your text Christologically. Remember, your exposition of the text must always emerge from a sound exegesis of your text.

Chapter eleven details how to bridge from the text to the sermon. We begin by identifying the primary theme of the text. Different scholars call this different terms, but essentially you are asking what is this text all about when you view it as a whole. Be able to put in writing what you see clearly as the text's primary theme. In this step, you are trying to identify what your text meant when it was first penned and what it means now by implication.

Chapter twelve on outlining the sermon takes the primary theme and divides it into parts that will reinforce the theme. Know that a well-constructed outline is essential. It is the best way to get the primary theme to come to life in the lives of the people to whom you preach.

In short, the outline will be to your sermon what the skeleton is to the body. As such, each outline will need three components: unity, balance, and movement. It is my contention that your outline, like your message, should be driven by the text, anchored in the text, and surface from the text. The latter part of this chapter will provide some guidelines on outlining your sermon.

Chapter thirteen reviews the art of illustrating your sermons. Whereas outlining your sermon is like creating a skeleton, illustrating it is like putting meat on the bones. In this chapter, we will examine what various scholars have suggested with respect to illustrating, as well as review some cautions. We will conclude with a set of suggestions for effective use of illustrations.

Even in this introduction, let me give you three insights. First, illustrations are everywhere, and you can train your mind to look for them. Second, never relate a story as though it were yours if it is not. And third, if an illustration sounds too good to be true, it probably is. Remember, people will remember your illustrations longer than they remember your points.

In my mind, I see illustrations as windows and mirrors. Windows let the light in so we can see clearly. Mirrors help us to see ourselves. Illustrations function the same way.

Chapter fourteen will address the matter of application. I agree with Spurgeon here that where the application begins the sermon begins and not before. Application links the truth of God's Word with the hearers' lives and needs.

John Broadus provides the classic definition of application. He says, "[It] in the strict sense, is that part, or those parts, of the discourse in which we show how the subject applies to the persons addressed, what practical instructions it offers them, what practical demands it makes upon them."[4]

I point out to my students that some sermons have no application. I would not call them sermons. Some sermons use application points as their main points. This is Rick Warren's model. Other sermons incorporate application at the conclusion of each major section. Adrian Rogers followed this model. Then again, many preachers historically placed the applications as the concluding section of their sermon. The Puritans followed this model. Jonathan Edwards was a practitioner of this style. My point is this: make sure your sermon has application for the hearer somewhere in your message. If you do not include application, you are not preaching. I will conclude this chapter with some guidelines for making effective applications.

---

4   John Broadus, *On the Preparation and Delivery of Sermons*, 3rd ed. Revised by J.B. Weatherspoon (New York: Harper and Brothers, 1944), 211.

Chapter fifteen addresses issues related to introducing and concluding the sermon, along with some suggestions for extending an effective invitation.

I tell my students that when they stand to preach, they have in the neighborhood of three to five minutes to gain the audience's attention. If they have not engaged the hearers by then, more than likely they have lost them. Here, we will examine some principles for making effective introductions.

The climax of the message should be its conclusion. Here, the preacher is pleading with the hearer to embrace and surrender to what God has said in His Word. In sales terms, the conclusion closes the deal so the listener is compelled to obey the Lord. At this point, the preacher addresses more than the mind and the emotions; he is addressing the will.

Effective preachers know how to transition seamlessly from their conclusion into an invitation. I have heard it said that the really great preachers actually begin their sermons by including mention of the invitation to come. This is a finely honed skill. Here we will consider some principles of extending an effective invitation. We will also address some of the stereotypes that critics have presented. Most, I believe, are proverbial straw men.

Chapter sixteen will review some guidelines of effective delivery. I have heard some great sermons delivered poorly. Anyone called to preach, I believe, can improve his or her delivery skills.

In this chapter, I will offer suggestions on how to become a more effective communicator. I will caution you against practicing the major mistakes that bore people. We have the most important message in the world, so let's communicate it with all the discipline and skill we can give.

The epilogue will provide some parting thoughts for the student of preaching.

My hope is that this volume will help you become the very best biblical preacher you can become.

Chapter 2

The Preacher as a Man of God

In the sovereignty and wisdom of Almighty God, the human destiny of the church, along with its unfolding of history, is dependent upon the men of God entrusted to proclaim the Word of God. Most evangelical historians agree that the church has been its strongest when its preaching has been its best. The progress of the gospel is staked upon those who proclaim it. Consider, then, the Scriptures' own counsel concerning this awesome responsibility.

As we make our way through the process of preparing to preach biblical messages, understand that it starts with the God-called preacher. My assumption is that God calls men to lead the local congregation and that the New Testament provides insight into the tasks that the God-called man must understand. Consider some of the New Testament terms used to describe the work.

New Testament Terms

In Acts 1:8, Jesus tells His disciples, "You shall be my *witnesses.*" I agree that this task is given to every believer, yet no one can endeavor to be a minister of the gospel who does not bear witness to what he has experienced. Whenever we stand to preach, we bear witness to who Christ is, what He has done, and what He can and will do in the life of the listener.

In Acts 20:17, we are told that Paul summoned the elders of the church in Ephesus. When they arrived, he exhorted them to be on guard for themselves and their flock (v. 28). The word *elder* comes from the word from which we get our word *Presbyterian*. By context, we understand that elders are assigned to give oversight (leadership) to the local church (v. 28). In the book of Acts, the tasks assigned to the apostles become the tasks assigned to the elders. From Acts 6, we conclude that the elders are to minister the Word (vv. 2, 4), pray (v. 4), and give leadership and oversight to the congregation (v. 36). Thus, the pastor and pastoral staff are the biblical elders in the local congregation.

In Acts 20:28, we see the word *overseers*. We get our word *episcopal* from this Greek word. It depicts the task that elders are to lead. It is also translated as bishops in 1 Timothy 3:1. The principal character quality of the overseer is that he is to be above reproach (1 Tim. 3:2). Here, he is assigned the task of taking care of the church of God (v. 5).

Again in Acts 20:28, we see another term, *shepherd*. We are to relate to the church as a shepherd relates to his flock. The word for shepherd is also translated "pastor." This word depicts the responsibility of caring for, providing for, and guarding the flock (church). Paul points out to the Ephesian elders (pastors) that they must protect the flock from those who attempt to attack and destroy the church.

In 1 Corinthians 1:21 and 23, the minister is identified as a *herald*. The noun form depicts one who makes a proclamation (or preaches) and the verb form one who is proclaiming or preaching. As Paul says, "We preach Christ." Central to the task of the minister is the responsibility to preach. The one distinguishing mark separating pastor and deacons is that the pastor must be "apt to teach" (1 Tim. 3:2); that is, he must be able to demonstrate communication skills.

In 1 Corinthians 3:5, the pastor is called a *minister*. This is also translated *"servant."* Interestingly, the Greek word is the same as our root word for deacon. As you read through the New Testament epistles, it is readily seen how often Paul and others refer to themselves in the salutations as "servants and apostles of Jesus Christ." I take the words *doulos* and *diakonos* to be synonyms with respect to intentions. Ministers are God's servants whose responsibility it is to carry out His agenda.

Another word for the ministerial task is that we are *"stewards"* (1 Cor. 4:1–2), although the term for servant in these verses is different and refers to the one who is in the service of another. The word he focuses on here is "steward." This word depicts one who is the manager of a household, one who has both great responsibility and great accountability. The principal responsibility is to be found faithful or trustworthy. Consider Jesus's assessment in the parable of the talents (Matt. 25:14–30).

In 1 Corinthians 4:14–15, Paul describes himself in terms of being a spiritual *"father."* He states, "For in Christ Jesus I became your father through the gospel." When you have the privilege of leading someone into the family of God, you play the role of a spiritual father. This term depicts the preacher's need to be loving and gentle. As a human father cares for his children, so spiritual fathers should care for those entrusted to their care.

In 2 Corinthians 5:11, Paul says, "We are ambassadors for Christ." While every Christian in a sense is an *ambassador* for Christ, the pastor must be keenly aware that he represents Jesus Christ in this world. As such, we have no liberty to craft our own agenda but must represent our Lord as He demands. When Paul writes in 1 Corinthians 11:23 that he has delivered to the believers what he has received from Christ, he is providing a perfect example of our task as an ambassador. We represent Christ's interests, not our own.

When Paul describes the leadership gifts in the church, he identifies the *pastor-teacher* (Eph. 4:11) as last in the sequence of gifted leaders. These terms, which most scholars identify as a hyphenated "pastor-teacher," depict one who is a shepherd who teaches. That is, he is one who cares for the church and has communication gifts for the church.

In the Pastoral Epistles, the minister is identified as a *"man of God"* (1 Tim. 6:11). We will return to this in a few paragraphs.

In 2 Timothy 2:24, the minister is identified as a *"slave of the Lord."* A slave is one who is owned by another, carries out the will of another, and is accountable to another.

The last term I draw your attention to is that the minister or pastor is identified as a *leader.* In Hebrews 13:7 and 17, the Scripture gives this admonition: "Remember your leaders who have spoken God's word to you. As you carefully observe the outcome of their lives, imitate their faith … Obey your leaders and submit to them, for they keep watch over your souls as those who will give an account, so that you can do this with joy and not with grief, for that would be unprofitable for you."

These New Testament terms provide a composite picture of the work of the local pastor. If your calling is to serve as a pastor, permit me to give you some advice as you undertake your calling.

A Challenge

First, I challenge you to make sure of your salvation. You will never be effective in ministry helping people come to faith or grow in faith if you are uncertain about your own faith. Paul said, "Everyone who calls upon the name of the Lord will be saved" (Rom. 10:13). John's prologue tells us, "But to all who did receive Him, He gave them the right to be children of God, even to those who believe upon His name" (John 1:12). So my question to you is: have you believed, and have you called upon the Lord? If the answer to that is yes, then trust the Lord that what He said is true and move forward in faith.

Second, make sure of your calling to ministry. I addressed this earlier in chapter one. One tangible way of knowing you are called to the ministry is that you have an absolute certainty that you cannot do anything else. In fact, if you can do anything else with respect to your vocation and still be content and satisfied, I recommend that you do it. Being in the ministry is not easy. It takes long hours and great patience. It is not uncommon for a pastor who is serving the Lord effectively to come under attack. In fact, Paul told Timothy to expect persecution. When the attacks come, many times the only reason you do not quit is because you know you are called.

Third, live by your priorities. I have heard it said that the person who fails to prioritize will live in the thick of thin things. So what are your priorities? As a pastor, you must maintain your relationship with the Lord, your family, and then your ministry—and in that order. If you are the senior pastor with preaching responsibilities, I challenge you to make that your first ministry priority. Set your priorities.

Fourth, control your calendar. I suspect that many people in your circle of influence have as their motto a hybrid of the first of the Four Spiritual Laws: "God loves you, and I have a wonderful plan for your life." If you do not protect your calendar, you will find yourself wasting your time and your life. I am not against being flexible when it is necessary—and I know what it is like to drop everything and head to the hospital for an emergency—but if you do not plan your time, it is easy to fritter it away with trivial matters. When planning your time, ask, what is it that God wants me to accomplish? Let that set your agenda! By the way, it is acceptable to say no. You do not have to accept every invitation. And you do not have to live trying to please people. Live your life for an audience of one!

Fifth, guard your time with God. No one is going to force you to have a quiet time, read through the Bible, or pray with intensity. In fact, people can and will make so many demands on you that you may see these disciplines being squeezed out of your life. I will give you the same caution I received years ago: do not get so busy in the work of the Kingdom that you neglect the King. Guard your time with God.

Sixth, guard your heart. When Solomon wrote to his son, he said, "Guard your heart above all else, for it is the source of life" (Prov. 4:23). Another translation says, "For out of it springs the issues of life." Sadly, Solomon did not practice what he preached, and as a result, it cost him dearly. If you fail to guard your heart, it may cost you dearly as well. Be careful where you go, what you do, what you see, and where you allow your mind to dwell. Notice the progression in Psalm 1:1: walking, standing, and sitting. What if Samson had guarded his heart? Or Gehazi? Or Uzziah? Perhaps their life stories would have been different. You decide what gets into your heart. Guard it.

Seventh, never forget that preparation precedes performance. One of my favorite sayings is, "Champions are made in the off season." When others are taking it easy and relaxing, the future champion is paying the price of preparation. I am a firm believer that God always prepares us before He uses us. It is the wise person who cooperates with the preparation. If you will think back to the story of David and Goliath in 1 Samuel 17, before David took on the giant, he had experience as he guarded his sheep in killing both the lion and the bear. In fact, verse 36 tells us that this happened on multiple occasions. No wonder he was ready for the giant! How can you prepare today for tomorrow's challenges? Consider Moses' forty years in the wilderness. Even though he thought that his life had been wasted, it was actually God's preparation for the greatest exodus in human history. The next time you are tempted to complain or criticize your circumstances, stop and ask, "Is this actually God's preparation?"

Eighth, become a student of the Word. If you are called to preach, you are called to preach God's Word. You cannot effectively communicate what you do not know. I advise my students, especially in their first five to ten years of ministry, to set aside at least two hours a day to read and study their Bible. Follow the example of the Psalmist (1:2) where we are told that "his delight is in the law of the Lord and in His law he meditates day and night." You cannot meditate on what is not there. Become a student of the Word.

Ninth, anticipate the fruit of a disciplined life. If you will work hard, pray hard, and practice self-discipline, I am convinced that God will honor your faithfulness. Remember, your goal is to be pleasing to Him. Remember Jesus' words from the Sermon on the Mount, "And your Father who sees in secret will reward you openly." Let me encourage you to reflect on Galatians 6:7, "Be not deceived, God is not mocked, for whatsoever a man sows that shall he also reap." We reap what we sow, more than we sow, later than we sow, and oftentimes others reap what we sow … for good or bad. Anticipate the fruit of a disciplined life.

Tenth, play to your strengths. God has gifted each of us with a different set of gifts, talents, passions, experiences, and maturity level. As you look at yourself, let me encourage you to work where you can be most effective. If you will think back to the story of David and Goliath, again, David could not, did not, and would not use Saul's armor and weapons. His assessment, was, "These are untested." So what did he do? He went to war with the familiar: a sling, a pouch with five smooth stones, and perhaps a staff. He played to his strengths, trusting for God's intervention, and walked away a hero.

Eleventh, walk by faith. Of course, this is easier said than done, particularly when life gets tough. If you think again to the David and Goliath story, David was the only one with a vertical perspective. Everyone else viewed life from the strictly horizontal. Goliath, Saul, the Israelite soldiers, Eliab; everyone looked at the crisis from a sight perspective. But when David walked on the scene, his was vertical. I notice that with David, faith overcomes fear, discouragement, criticism, and one very big giant. I challenge you to place your gaze on God and your glance at the circumstances. Trust God, and expect God to work in and through your life.

Twelfth, love the people you serve. You will need to demonstrate this in what you do. At times, you will need to tell them. One way you will demonstrate your love is simply by being present. Remember, love is more than an emotion. It is a commitment. If you love God, you can love the people He has called you to pastor. Let me inject one word of counsel. The larger the congregation you serve, the more you move from being a shepherd to a rancher where you must delegate ministry responsibilities. Do you really think that on Pentecost, Peter dealt with all three thousand converts personally? When Paul was unable to go himself, he sent someone. And if there was no one to send, he sent letters. In a day where communication technology has skyrocketed, you certainly can keep in touch. Recall the earlier advice: people do not care how much you know until they know how much you care. When necessary, get help ministering to people.

The Man of God

As I wrote earlier, one title for a minister that stands out is that we are "men of God." It is one of the great descriptive declarations about a preacher. He is God's man. Paul writes to Timothy and says, "You are

God's man." This is an incredible privilege. Although Timothy is the only New Testament figure called "God's man," it is a common designation for Old Testament leaders. Moses, Samuel, Elijah, Elisha, David, and a host of others are called men of God.

His Identity

From the context in 1 Timothy 6:11–14, God's man is called to communicate God's Word. Timothy finds himself in a very elite company. Of course, 2 Timothy 3:17 extends this identity to all who preach the Word. Paul's point to Timothy is that he is no longer the world's man or his own man; he is God's man, God's property, God's possession. In marking the identity of a man of God, Paul tells Timothy that the man of God displays four qualities.

First, he is identified by what he *flees* from (v. 11a). I have seen this outline used on numerous occasions by numerous preachers and commentators. John MacArthur did a fine job in his exposition of this text. These "things" in verse 11 refer to the love of money (vv. 9–10), immorality (1 Cor. 6:18), idolatry (1 Cor. 10:14), and pride (1 Tim. 3:6). In fact, the word flee has the root word for fugitive. Be a fugitive from these things. The primary reference, however, is to the love of money. In Jesus' words, you cannot serve God and mammon (money).[5]

Second, the man of God is identified by what he *follows* after (v. 11b). Here, Paul gives Timothy six character qualities to pursue. In short, Paul says, this is your agenda: pursue righteousness. By context, we know this is practical righteousness. It is doing the right thing in the sight of God and man. It is outward in its orientation. Next, Paul tells Timothy to pursue godliness. In contrast, this is inward. It is living in the light of God's presence. Paul uses this term nine times in the Pastoral Epistles. These two overarching terms describe the essence of Christian character. Paul says pursue these things. Graham Scroggie wrote, "God calls us to co-operate with Him in the perfecting of character."[6] After the first two qualities, Paul says we are to likewise pursue faith; that is, trust the Lord in all things. We are to pursue love. This is to both God and our fellow human beings (Matt. 22:34–40). We are to pursue endurance. This is the word meaning to bear up under the load and is often translated as "patience." It is a loyalty that refuses to quit. And finally, we are to pursue gentleness. This dictates

---

5   John MacArthur, "The Man of God and Expository Preaching" in *Rediscovering Expository Preaching*, ed. John MacArthur (Dallas: Word Publishing, 1992), 85–101.
6   John Blanchard, ed., *Gathered Gold* (Hertfordshire: Evangelical Press, 1984), 26.

how we relate to people. All of these things, Paul says, we are to pursue. The man of God is identified by what he follows after.

Next, the man of God is identified by what he *fights* for (v. 12). Paul tells us that we must be warriors. Being in the ministry is like being at war. The enemies of the world, the flesh, the devil, and the carnal are constant. The word "fight" comes from the root word from which we get the term *agony*. And we are to fight the good fight for the faith. With all of the effort we can expend, we are to advance God's agenda and God's kingdom. Do this, Paul says, in light of eternity.

Last, the man of God is identified by what he is *faithful* to (vv. 13–14). Here is a solemn charge to keep God's Word without compromise until the return of Christ. Paul tells Timothy, live in such a way that your life is pleasing to God. Here is a picture of God's man. The charge Paul gave to Timothy is ours as well. Here is the man of God's identity.

His Journey

Paul also writes about the man of God's journey (2 Tim. 3:14–4:5). On this journey, Paul tells Timothy that the Word of God is his authority (vv. 14–16). He says continue in what you have learned and firmly believe. This word "continue" is translated "remain" or "abide." Paul states that the sacred writings are able to instruct him for salvation through faith in Christ. The Word of God itself is a means of grace. Paul points out that all Scripture is inspired by God and is profitable for teaching, rebuke, correcting, and training in righteousness.

Paul goes on to say not only is the Word of God your authority, but being a man of God should also be your priority (v. 17). The Word is given for the purpose of the man of God becoming complete so that he will be equipped for every good work. Note that Paul cites the place of good works fourteen times in the Pastoral Epistles.

Paul then declares to Timothy that preaching is his instrumentality (vv. 1–5). I charge you, he says to Timothy, preach the Word! He is to preach when it is convenient and inconvenient. He is to rebuke, correct, and encourage with great patience. Paul tells him that a time is coming when people will not want to hear. Preach anyway. And do not give up.

His Equipping

Permit me to offer a few thoughts on the man of God's equipping. Consider the summary statement concerning Jesus found in Luke 2:52,

"And Jesus kept on increasing in wisdom and stature and in favor with God and man." Can you agree with me that Jesus is our supreme role model for Christian ministry? Our task is to be like Him, be filled with Him, serve Him, live for Him, and if need be, die for Him. So, how are we to be like Jesus?

First, like Him, we are to make progress. We are told here that Jesus "kept on increasing." This is a word that describes a pioneer making progress through a forest or a jungle. It is progress made through diligent effort. It is a balanced progress. Jesus increased first in wisdom. This is the ability to see life from God's perspective. In His self-emptying, Jesus had to grow in wisdom. It is knowledge and the ability to apply it. It implies mental, emotional, and volitional development. Was it not Augustine who said, "The Holy Spirit has an affinity for a man with a trained mind"? In the words of John Stott, your mind matters.

Jesus also grew in stature. This depicts physical development. It implies that we need to take care of ourselves physically. George Whitefield said, "I would rather burn out than rust out." He did; in 1770 at the ripe old age of fifty-six. In contrast, John Wesley took care of himself physically. He died in 1791 at the age of eighty-eight. He had thirty-two more years of productive ministry than Whitefield.

Next, Jesus increased in favor with God. The Son of God in His self-limitation grew spiritually. Although He was (and is) God in the flesh, He did not circumvent the need to have a steady intake of the Word, the necessity of prayer, and a consistent walk of obedience and dependence upon His Heavenly Father. Seminary can sharpen your mind, but you must take responsibility to grow spiritually.

Jesus also grew in favor with His fellow man. He grew socially. He learned to relate to people, and we must do the same. Your life's ministry will be with people, so learn to love people now! Like Jesus, we need to make progress.

Again, I want to reiterate the God who wants us to progress also wants us prepared. That truth was preeminent with Jesus. He had thirty years of preparation and then three and a half years of public ministry. Without fail, God prepares us before He uses us. Moses took forty years in the wilderness. Joshua was Moses's understudy. Peter the fisherman became Peter the fisher of men. John, who first surfaces as mending the nets, is called to mend the nets of a torn church and theology with his gospel, epistles, and Revelation. Paul the passionate persecutor becomes the passionate evangelist. Each of these men was prepared before they were used. Part of our preparation is that we cultivate a sense of expectancy. William Carey wrote, "Attempt great things for God, expect great things from God."

Advice for the Man of God

In order for you to make progress and be prepared for how God will use you, I want to challenge you to give keen attention to your own performance. Consider these eight focal points as reminders.

First, focus on people. They are your ministry. Scripture tells us that when Jesus saw the multitudes, He was moved with compassion. We are told that He wept over Jerusalem. Yet, He did not bat an eye when He spoke of the Temple's destruction. Why? He came to die for people. That was His ministry. You, too, must focus on people.

Second, I challenge you to focus on your purpose. Why are you here? What does God want to accomplish through your life? Ask Him to clarify it for you. Jesus knew His purpose. He came to seek and save the lost and destroy the works of the devil. He came that we might have life and have it more abundantly. He came to go to Calvary! So, why are you here? Ask the Lord to clarify that in your heart and mind.

Third, I say again (and I cannot say this enough), live by your priorities. Jesus knew what was most important, and He gave Himself to those things. When He came to the end of His earthly life prior to the cross, He could say, "Father I have accomplished the work You gave Me to do." Again, I challenge you to live by your priorities.

Fourth, I want to encourage you to focus on productivity. Jesus said, "Of those you gave Me I have lost none."(John 18:9). I challenge you to pray about your ministry until you know what God wants done. Then work with all of your sanctified might to accomplish God's will for your life.

Fifth, work within your parameters. In other words, bloom where you are planted. Where God places you, work with all your heart. Jesus never reviled the High Priest or resorted to tearing down synagogues. He worked within the system where the Father placed Him. I encourage you to work within the system where God has placed you. The best change comes from the inside out.

Sixth, give yourself to prayer and preaching. Jesus said, "Whatever you ask in prayer believing you shall receive"(Matthew 21:22). Paul talked about how it pleased God through the foolishness of preaching to save those who believe. Recall how the disciples asked Jesus to teach them to pray. When tempted to get sidetracked because of real, pressing needs, the apostles said, "It is not desirable for us to neglect the Word of God ... But we will devote ourselves to prayer, and to the ministry of the Word" (Acts 6:2a, 4). If it was of critical importance for them, it is of critical importance for us.

Seventh, insist on purity. First Thessalonians 4:3 says, "For this is the will of God, even our sanctification." The great problem with the Pharisees was that they looked good outwardly but were corrupt and empty inwardly. Recall the words of Robert Murray McCheyne as he preached the ordination of Dan Edwards in the 1860s:

> Mr. Edwards ... do not forget the inner man, the heart. The cavalry officer knows that his life depends upon his saber, so he keeps it clean. Every stain he wipes off with the greatest care. Mr. Edwards you are God's chosen instrument. According to your purity, so shall be your success. It is not great talent; it is not great ideas that God uses, it is great likeness to Jesus Christ. Mr. Edwards, a holy man is an awesome weapon in the hand of God.[7]

McCheyne is right. It is God's will for you to be holy, pure, sanctified, and useful.

Finally, depend upon God for power. The result of purity is power. If you will put these things into practice, I believe you can experience the anointing and glory of God in your ministry.

The question keeps coming up. Why are there so many Christian ministers who are not experiencing the anointing and glory and power of God in their lives? I can think of no reason other than the simple fact that they are content to live without it!

As a preacher, I challenge you to be God's man.

---

7   Paraphrase of Andrew Bonar, ed, *Memoirs of McCheyne* (Chicago: Moody Press, reprinted 1978), 95.

Chapter 3

The Role of Hermeneutics and Sermon Preparation

As we begin the task of preparing to preach the Word of God, we must understand that it is not our prerogative to distort, deny, or denigrate its teaching. Our task is to understand its content, embody its principles, and communicate it as heaven's counsel for the present moment.

Before delving into the details of Bible interpretation, I want to share with you some preliminary principles of sermon preparation. Assuming that you will be preaching on a regular basis, I want to share with you some lessons that need to be learned early.

Lessons Learned

First, preparing to preach requires getting into a discipline and a rhythm. The only way you can consistently preach sound biblical messages over a long period of time is to cultivate a disciplined approach to preparation. If you preach one, two, or three new messages a week, it will take time for you to prepare. You can only go to past files and sugar sticks so long before they run dry. In my last pastorate, I averaged preaching either two or three new messages a week. This would have been impossible apart from a disciplined approach to preparation, and that on multiple levels.

Second, preparing to preach requires developing a method of preparation. For me, that meant planning ahead. Sometime between Thanksgiving and New Year's each year, I would block off a week and plan my preaching for the coming year. I would identify series, titles, and texts.

I would have file folders made up with the planned messages in sequence. I would have commentaries, texts, and lexical aids copied and placed in the folders. In short, I would not have to start from scratch each week. I will say more about this process in a later chapter.

Starting from scratch on Monday morning, trying to decide what to preach on next Sunday, is an almost impossible task. Those who rely on this method often rely on what I call the "Saturday night special" approach to preparation. No wonder these sermons on the whole are substandard. The only preacher I know of who relied successfully on this methodology was Charles Spurgeon, and he was a unique case. He averaged reading a book a day, spent somewhere in the neighborhood of eight to ten hours a day in his study, and had a near photographic memory. If you have these qualities, then you can probably start from scratch each week as he did. If you do not, like most of us, I suggest you plan ahead. It is the "work smarter not harder" principle.

I was always keenly aware that Sunday was on the way. No matter what I did, I could not slow down the clock or the calendar. On Monday, I would spend most of my working day, usually eight to ten hours or more, working on my sermon(s) for the coming Sunday. I would work through the texts, and my goal for the day was to finish my exegesis of the texts for the messages and establish a preliminary outline for the sermons. Where I pastored, we had morning and evening services where I preached two different messages each Sunday. As a rule, I preached the same sermon multiple times on Sunday morning and a different one in the evening.

On Tuesday, I had my worship team meeting. In this meeting, we reviewed the past Sunday's services, asking the questions: What went right? What went wrong? How can we improve? What should we have done differently? We thoroughly critiqued the services. Next, I would pass out my outlines of the coming Sunday's sermons and would teach it to my team much like a small group Bible study. Then, I would solicit feedback. I was looking for insights, age-appropriate applications, and even some suggested illustrations. After this part, my musicians would tell us what they planned to do with respect to music next Sunday. They can do this when they know the series, themes, titles, and texts months in advance. Periodically, we would spend time discussing how to package and promote upcoming series. After closing with a time of prayer, we would usually have lunch together.

After other meetings on Tuesday, I would revise my outlines if I thought it necessary. By the end of Tuesday, I would have my final outlines in hand. The rest of the week I spent looking for illustrations. No later than Thursday, I would have my final outlines to the office, where we would print interactive outline notes to be distributed at Sunday's services. In short, this is my method. For me, preparing to preach requires developing a method. For the record, I would usually paperclip the outline of my sermons into my Bible before I preached. The key to having notes is not being tied to them.

Third, and back to sermon preparation, the key to interpreting the text is learning to ask the right questions. In Robinson and Larson's anthology, *The Art and Craft of Biblical Preaching*, several chapters are given to asking the right questions. [8] The student should ask, what is the genre? What is the context? Are there semantic questions that need to be addressed? What is the principal theme of this text? What is the meaning of the individual words? How do the phrases in the text connect? What does the text mean for today's hearer? We will come back to these questions in more detail later. For now, understand that the preacher, like an investigator, must ask questions of the text in the search for meaning and understanding.

Fourth, as you prepare your messages, the steps you follow will eventually become second nature. Pilots follow a very specific written checklist. Specialists in the medical field follow a carefully detailed set of questions and steps. As you prepare your messages, the steps that you follow will eventually become second nature. You may or may not follow a written checklist, but you will follow a reasoned and logical set of steps.

Fifth, in the ministry you can delegate a lot of things, but you cannot delegate the things that only you can do. I believe that preaching and preparation for it are tops on your priority list. You cannot have someone else do your homework. That is not to say that you do not get assistance and feedback. You must take responsibility to prepare your own messages.

Asking the Right Questions

In sermon preparation, we start with the discipline of hermeneutics. Hermeneutics is defined as the art and science of biblical interpretation. In hermeneutics, we are asking what does this text say? And what does this text mean? Before giving attention to the process of preparation and the implementation of your hermeneutics model, consider some general principles with respect to interpretation.

---

8   Craig Brian Larson and Haddon Robinson, eds., *The Art and Craft of Biblical Preaching* (Grand Rapids: Zondervan, 2005), 230–41.

My first question is what genre am I dealing with? Is this prose? Is it poetry? Is it historical narrative? Is it Wisdom literature? Is it Apocalyptic literature? Is this a prophetic passage? Is this a parable or an extended metaphor? By identifying the genre first, you will know which tools to bring to your investigation.[9]

Second, what is the historic context? We must do our best to understand the condition of the day in which the text was written. By understanding the setting, you are more likely to grasp nuances and allusions. For example, Paul's references to cutting women's hair and eating meat offered to idols had specific references in first-century Corinth. Or when Jesus told His disciples to go the second mile, everyone understood the Roman law context.

Third, the contextual principle helps the student identify the place of the text in its larger context. When Jesus asked His disciples, "Who do men say that I the Son of Man am?" in Ceasarea Philippi, He was not having an identity crisis. Caesarea Philippi was a hotbed of multiple world and regional religions. Jesus asked the question in order to elicit Peter's response, thus confirming that Jesus was more than just one among many (Matt. 16:13–23). Or consider Jesus's parables of the lost sheep, the lost silver, and the lost son from Luke 15. The context demonstrates that this was Jesus's commentary on the grumbling of the Pharisees and scribes (vv. 1–2). Every time we select a text from which to preach, we should ask, what is the context?

Next, I consider the text proper. What is its dominant theme? Robinson calls this "the big idea." What stands out as the one overarching and distinct theme? What does the text say about this theme? If I, for example, preach on Matthew 6:5–15, the theme is prayer. Jesus assumes that we will pray. He is here teaching us principles to make us more effective in our prayers.

The next principle focuses attention on the linguistic issues. What is the meaning of the words or groups of words? For example, if I am preaching from Romans 1:18 and read about the wrath of God, the question should arise, what is the word for "wrath"? It is *orgay* and not *thumos*. What is the significance in this choice of words? And what does that tell us about the nature of God?

We should also consider the theological principle. Here, we seek (like the historic principle) to understand the people's line of understanding

---

9   See Jerry Vines and Jim Shaddix, *Power in the Pulpit* (Chicago: Moody Press, 1999), 100.

when they first heard this Scripture. The people of the Old Testament era did not see themselves as people under the New Covenant. What Moses permitted due to the hardness of man's heart, Jesus strictly forbade except under unique and strict circumstances.

Next is the practical principle. What should I know or believe based upon this passage? Is there a truth to embrace? A sin to confess? A promise to claim? A discipline to engage? A new insight into God's ways? Is there an example to follow? Is there a warning to heed?

Finally, there are some particular or specific principles that will apply based upon the genre, context, and intention. Some passages are to be taken literally. Others are figurative. A few are to be viewed allegorically because that is how they were intended. See, for example, Galatians 4:21–31.

These are a set of principles that provide the primary framework for our quest to interpret our text. So, let's now turn our attention to the process of sermon preparation as we use the hermeneutic tools to pull together our exegesis. Make note that the term "exegesis" means what I pull out of the text and not what I read into the text.

The Process

Whenever I speak to any group, I begin by asking three questions: Who am I speaking to? What are their needs? And what does God say? The discipline of hermeneutics addresses this third question. Our approach and process of hermeneutics revolves around three key questions. What does the text say? What does the text mean? What do I do in light of the text? This can be put simply as "What?" "So what?" and "Now what?"

In "what?" I am seeking to understand what the text says. Vines and Shaddix identify this stage as investigation. We are unable to determine what the text means until we determine what the text says. I suggest to my students that they read the text from which they are preaching anywhere from fifteen to twenty-five times in order to grasp what it says.

The process begins with a background study. How does the text from which I am preaching fit into the whole of Scripture? And how does it fit into the book in which it is located?

As we build a bridge from the then to the now, ask questions concerning the context. Who is the author or speaker? When was it written? For example, if you are preaching through 1 John, you will want to understand the issues relating to Gnosticism and the word "know." What is the setting? Is it a unique literary genre? Is there some special interest that sheds light on the text before us? In short, you want to gain a firm grasp of what this text says.

In "so what?" you are moving to interpretation. You want to know, "What does this text mean?" W. T. Connor is famous for saying, "The Bible does not mean what it says. It means what it means." For example, when Jesus said, "You are the salt of the earth," He was not saying you have become sodium chloride. He is saying that you the believer function the same way in society that salt functions in its environment. That is what it means. What the text says and what the text means are not always the same.

To minimize subjectivity, we examine the historic, contextual, syntactical, and linguistic issues. Walter Kaiser suggests that we do a "grammatical-contextual-historic-syntactical-theological-cultural exegesis." With this, we study the context and consider how each verse connects. Consider, for example, John 3:1–7. How does each verse connect? Is verse 5 not explained by verse 6? Is this not an example of Hebrew parallelism? Ask the question, how does my text fit in with the larger context? And how does the flow of the text unfold?[10]

Next, look for logical divisions in the text. What are the sequential thought patterns? How does the text unfold?

Follow this with your word studies. What words do you need to identify? What nouns are used? What verbs are used? Are any critical prepositions present? For example, *hina* in the Greek text introduces a purpose clause and should always be given serious consideration.

If you are able to read your text in the Hebrew and Greek, you will be ahead of the one who cannot. Grasp the meaning of the words as used in context. Be aware of any figures of speech. How often is a key word used in the Bible? With my Greek New Testament, my favorite tool is Fritz Rienecker's *A Linguistic Key to the Greek New Testament.*[11]

Next, check cross references. Here, we allow Scripture to interpret and shed light on Scripture. The best tool in this area is *A Treasury of Scripture Knowledge.* What other texts shed light on the text before you? At this point, the student should be coming to grips not only with what the text says but also with what it means.

The third step in the process is, "Now what?" Here, we are attempting to identify the timeless message from the text that will be applied specifically

---

10   Walter Kaiser, presentation at the Evangelical Theological Society, New Orleans, La., November, 2009.

11   Fritz Rienecker, *A Linguistic Key to the Greek New Testament.* 2 volumes. (Grand Rapids: Zondervan, 1976).

to the hearers. Answer these questions: What demands are being made on the believer or the unbeliever? What purpose is God revealing? What standards is God establishing? What theological truths are we being urged to embrace? As we examine the implications, diligently look for the timeless truths. Ask questions. Ask the Spirit to show you how this text applies to the people to whom you are preaching.

As you walk through the text, expend the energy, the effort, and the time to understand what it says, what it means, and what it demands.

Chapter 4

What Is Biblical Preaching?

When I have worked my way through the hermeneutics process, the end result for me is an exegesis of the text. As I begin to work on pulling together my sermon, I will use my exegesis and my Bible. These will be on the table before me, along with a legal pad and pen. Many preachers do their work off a computer. I do not. I prefer to have pen in hand. I think better that way.

As I begin to think and pray about the message I am preparing, it is wise to stop and ask the obvious question. What am I doing? In short, I am attempting to prepare myself and the message I intend to preach. At this juncture, it is also wise to clarify just exactly what I am attempting to accomplish. If I begin my process with the end result before me, I know that I am ultimately attempting to prepare and preach a biblical sermon. What exactly is a biblical sermon? And what is biblical preaching? First, review with me some of the biblical words for preaching. Next, students of preaching, historically, have provided numerous descriptions and definitions of the preaching task. Consider what these homileticians have written in the past. Then, permit me to offer my own definition of biblical preaching.

Biblical Terms for the Preaching Task

The New Testament provides several distinctive words to describe the preaching task. The first word, translated in context "tell you this good news" (Luke 1:19), depicts preaching as bringing or declaring good news. This word is used often in the New Testament.

A second word describes a herald or announcer. In Matthew 3:1, John the Baptist came "preaching in the wilderness." This role sees the preacher making public declarations as God's spokesman. In 2 Timothy 4:2, it is translated "preach the Word" or "proclaim the message."

In Acts 9:27, another word for our task is translated "to preach boldly" or "speak boldly." These principal words, verbs, describe the task of preaching.

The noun form describes the substance of the act of preaching. In Matthew 12:41, Jesus said, "The men of Ninevah will stand up at the judgment with this generation and condemn it, because they repented at Jonah's proclamation ..." And at times, the word *word* is used as in 1 Corinthians 1:18, "the word of the cross." This is not so much the act of preaching as it is the content of the message preached. Specifically, the preacher communicates God's Word, not his own speculative thoughts.

The most common name given for the preacher in the Bible is "herald." As Paul wrote to Timothy, he gave this confession, "For this I was appointed a herald, an apostle (I am telling the truth; I am not lying), and a teacher of the Gentiles in faith and truth" (1 Tim. 2:7).

As the student reflects on the importance of the preaching task, consider reading through the Pastoral Epistles. Here, the text contains over fifty references to the task of communication assigned to the preacher.

If the task of preaching, proclaiming, heralding, and communication is important, what specifically is it that we are called to do?

Definitions of Biblical Preaching

Throughout history, preachers and scholars have attempted to articulate the essence of preaching. Consider some of the following attempts at defining the task.

The first homiletics textbook that is still extant is Augustine's *On Christian Doctrine.* The text is divided into four books. The first three address hermeneutic issues. The fourth book attends to the details of crafting and delivering the sermon. It describes Augustine's assessment of the components of preaching: "There are two things in which all interpretations of Scripture demands: the mode of ascertaining the proper meaning, and the mode of making known the meaning." For the preacher, Augustine contends, both wisdom and eloquence are of great importance.

In brief, for Augustine, preaching is the art and craft of interpreting Scripture clearly and communicating it effectively. [12]

Citing Cicero, Augustine explains concerning the latter component:

> Accordingly a great orator has truly said that "an eloquent man must speak so as to teach, to delight and to persuade." Then he adds: "to teach is a necessity, to delight is a beauty, to persuade is a triumph." Now of these three, the one first mentioned, the teaching, which is a matter of necessity, depends on what we say; the other two on the way we say it. He, then, who speaks with the purpose of teaching should not suppose that he has said what he has to say as long as he is not understood; for although what he has said be intelligible to himself, it is not said at all to the man who does not understand it. If, however, he is understood, he has said his say, whatever may have been his manner of saying it. But if he wishes to delight or persuade his hearer as well, he will not accomplish that end by putting his thought in any shape no matter what, but for that purpose the style of speaking is a matter of importance. And as the hearer must be pleased in order to secure his attention, so he must be persuaded in order to move him to action. [13]

For John Calvin, preaching and prophesying were similar. In his commentary in 1 Thessalonians 5:20, he wrote, "By the term prophesying I do not mean the gift of foretelling the future, but as in 1 Corinthians 14:3 the science of the interpretation of Scripture, so that a prophet is the interpreter of the divine will...Let us understand prophesying to mean the interpretation of Scripture applied to the present need." In his commentary on Zechariah, Calvin notes, "Of course God wishes to be heard when he speaks through his servants and those whom he has made teachers." In his commentary on the Psalms, Calvin wrote, "For what is the purpose of the preaching of the Word, of the sacraments, of religious gatherings, and of the whole external order of the church except to unite us to God?" [14]

---

12 Augustine, *On Christian Doctrine*, Vol 18 in the Great Books of the Western World series, Robert M. Hutchings, ed. (Chicago: Encyclopedia Brittanica, 1952), 675, 677.

13 Ibid., 683–84.

14 John Calvin, *Epistle of Paul to the Roman and Thessalonians*, Ross Mackenzie, tr. (Grand Rapids: Wm. B. Eerdmans, 1960), 376; John Calvin, *Calvin: Commentaries*, Joseph Haroutunian, ed (Philadelphia: The Westminster Press, 1958), 387, 393.

If we take these three passages together, we can conclude with Calvin that preaching is the communication of divine truth by a God-called preacher who speaks on behalf of God from the Scriptures rightly interpreted and appropriately applied with the view of uniting the hearers to God.

The Classics of Faith and Devotion series of volumes includes *Evangelical Preaching* by Charles Simeon (1758–1836). According to the series' editors, he was the first preacher of the Church of England who endeavored to instruct ministers on how to prepare and deliver sermons. The editors noted that Simeon had "three aims in his preaching: to instruct, to please, and to affect his audience." Here, one can clearly see the influence of Augustine on Simeon. [15]

Two other influences on Simeon were Richard Baxter and George Herbert. In Baxter's *The Reformed Pastor*, about preaching, he states that it requires, "skill necessary to make plain the truth, to convince the hearers, to let the irresistible light into their consciences, and to keep it there and drive all home; to screw the truth into their minds and work Christ into their affections ... This should be done with a great deal of holy skill." George Herbert, in his classic *The Country Parson,* asserts "there are two things in sermons—the one informing, and the other inflaming." [16]

John Newton, slave trader turned preacher, said, "My grand point in preaching is to break the hard heart, and to heal the broken one." [17]

Charles Spurgeon, known as the Prince of Preachers in the golden Victorian age of preaching, penned for us a collection of addresses presented to the Pastor's College. Entitled *Lectures to My Students*, Spurgeon discusses numerous issues related to ministry but gives the bulk of attention to preaching. In his lecture, "Sermons—Their Matter," he quotes Gouge's summary description of preaching: "Ministers are herein to imitate God, and to their best endeavour, to instruct people in the mysteries of godliness, and to teach them what to believe and practice, and then to stir them up to act and deed, to do what they are instructed to do." [18]

In his classic textbook on preaching, *On the Preparation and Delivery of Sermons,* John Broadus stated, "the great appointed means of spreading the good tidings of salvation through Christ is preaching—words spoken to the individual or to the assembly." He says later, "The subject of preaching

---

15   Charles Simeon, *Evangelical Preaching* (Portland: Multnomah Press, 1986), XVII.
16   Ibid.,
17   Blanchard, 233.
18   Charles H. Spurgeon, *Lectures to My Students* (Grand Rapids: Zondervan, 1987), 71.

is divine truth, centrally the gospel as revealed and offered in Jesus Christ. Its object is eternal life …" [19]

Broadus quotes Phillips Brooks' classic definition of preaching: "Preaching," wrote Brooks, "is the communication of truth by man to men. It has in it two essential elements, truth and personality. Neither of those can it spare and still be preaching. It must have both elements." [20]

Another classic definition of preaching is offered by T. Harwood Pattison in his *The Making of the Sermon*. He states:

> Preaching is the spoken communication of divine truth with a view to persuasion. Accepting this as a sufficient definition, we notice that it covers three points with which we are chiefly concerned in a sermon, namely: its matter, its manner, and its purpose. As to the matter of this communication, it is "divine truth." This tells us what to preach. As to the manner of this communication, it is divine truth "spoken." This tells us how to preach. As to the purpose of this communication, it is divine truth spoken "with a view to persuasion." This tells us why we preach. [21]

In their anthology *The Art and Craft of Biblical Preaching*, the compilers, Craig Brian Larson and Haddon Robinson, include essays from a variety of homiletic scholars. Many of these writers offer definitions and descriptions of preaching.

John Stott gives this definition of biblical exposition (his term for preaching): "to expound Scripture is to open up the inspired text with such faithfulness and sensitivity that God's voice is heard and his people obey him."[22]

Jay Kesler provides a brief description of preaching which he says, in essence, it "is an appeal to the will." Crawford Loritts likewise provides a succinct definition: "It is a word from God for the people at a moment in history." [23]

Jeffrey Arthurs says, "The Bible's portrayal of preaching is best caught with a general term like biblical communication or speaking on behalf of

---

19 Broadus, 3, 6.

20 Ibid., 5.

21 T. Harwood Pattison, *The Making of the Sermon* (Philadelphia: The American Baptist Publication Society, 1941), 3.

22 John Stott, "A Definition of Biblical Preaching," in Larson and Robinson, 24.

23 Jay Kesler, "Overfed, Underchallenged," in Larson and Robinson, 31; Crawford Loritts, "Preaching that Raises Our Sights," in Larson and Robinson, 36

God." He further notes that "John Stott's phrase 'standing between two worlds' summarizes this ministry."[24]

Hadden Robinson provides his classic definition of preaching. He notes, "Expository preaching [which he equates with biblical preaching] is the communication of a biblical concept, derived from and transmitted through historical, grammatical, and literary study of a passage in its context, which the Holy Spirit first applies to the personality and experience of the preacher, then through the preacher applies to the hearer."[25]

Chuck Smith, founder of the Calvary Chapel movement, cites Nehemiah 8:8 where the text says, "They read from the Book of the Law of God, making it clear and giving the meaning so that the people could understand what was being read." His assessment is "that is as good a description of expository teaching (preaching) as you can find. They read the Word, making it clear." He then notes, "They gave the meaning and caused the people to understand it." [26]

John Koessler writes, "The preacher's task is always to explain, prove, or apply the biblical author's idea in its context." Using Jonathan Edwards as an example, he observes, "His sermons ... even his most revivalistic ones, were carefully constructed monuments to biblical exegesis, as they followed the tripartite scheme of clarifaction of biblical text, elaboration of doctrine implicit in the text, and application of text and doctrine to the lives of his hearers."[27]

Alluding to William Perkins' descriptions of the preaching task, D. A. Carson asserts that our aim as preachers is "to take the sacred text, explain what it means, tie it to other Scriptures so people can see the whole a little better, and apply it to life so it bites and heals, instructs and edifies." [28]

These are but a sample of the collective wisdom through history of descriptions and definitions of the preaching task. Hopefully, this will assist students in their broader understanding of the preaching task.

A Definition of Biblical Preaching

Biblical preaching is the event of verbally communicating a message that is rooted in Scripture by a spokesman representing God to either

---

24 Jeffrey Arthurs, "Preaching Life into the Church," in Larson and Robinson, 54.
25 Haddon Robinson, "My Theory of Homiletics," in Larson and Robinson, 58.
26 Chuck Smith, "The Power of Simplicity," in Larson and Robinson, p 121.
27 John Koessler, "Why All the Best Preachers Are Theological," in Larson and Robinson, 243, 245.
28 D.A. Carson, "Teaching the Whole Bible," in Larson and Robinson, 404.

believers (for the purpose of communicating His truth, reproof, correction, and instruction), or to unbelievers (with a view to their conversion or judgment) with the ultimate intention of bringing all hearers into Christian maturity and the culture into Christian conformity.

When Stephen Covey wrote his *Seven Habits of Highly Effective People*, he essentially communicated a set of principles that achievers embrace. One principle, a habit, states, "Begin with the end in mind." Know at the outset what you are trying to accomplish. If we will keep this simple principle in mind, I am convinced that it will help us be more effective preachers. Consider, then, the six components of biblical preaching. Here is what we are aiming to embrace.[29]

First, biblical preaching is an event of verbally communicating a message. When we consider the dimensions of time, we consider process and events, process being the unfolding or passing of time. Event is similar to *kairos* or special, significant moments in time. When Jesus responded to the apostles' inquiry, "Is it at this time that you are restoring the kingdom to Israel?" He said, "It is not for you to know the times or the seasons" (*chronos* and *kairos*). "Seasons" is translated variously as "periods, eras, occasions, or opportunities." Again, it depicts special moments in the unfolding of time. These points are events.

I recall hearing Jerry Rankin say, "Only in the present does time touch eternity." And it is in the present moment of preaching that God supernaturally communicates through the preaching of the Word.

As we study the Scriptures, we see repeatedly how God communicates His Word through a verbal communication of the message. Recall how Joshua said, "Choose for yourselves this day whom you will serve ... as for me and my house, we will serve the Lord" (Josh. 24:15). Or consider Elijah's showdown with the prophets of Baal (1 Kings 18), or Nathan's confrontation with King David after David sinned grievously (2 Sam. 12). When Jesus preached His Sermon on the Mount, or when Peter preached on Pentecost, or when Paul preached at Mars Hill, each of these events happened in a specific time and place. Preaching occurs in time and space. It is an event of verbally communicating God's message. And that message reveals the heart, mind, and will of God.

Second, biblical preaching is rooted in Scripture. I teach my students that biblical sermons are anchored in the text, driven by the text, and surface from the text. If not, it is not biblical preaching.

---

29 See Stephen Covey, *Seven Habits of Highly Effective People* (New York: Free Press, 1990), Habit 2.

My conclusion, based on the witness of Romans 10, is that the communication of the Word of God is the Lord's primary means of extending grace. In this sense, preaching is a traditional fulfillment of the classic idea of a sacrament.

In preaching, what is critical is not our opinions or preferences but what God says. That being the case, preachers have an obligation to emulate the words of Paul in 1 Corinthians 11:23, "What I have received from the Lord, I have delivered unto you." Much like a server in a restaurant, the preacher's obligation is to get the spiritual food from the place of preparation to those who are hungry to eat. We have no right to alter the meal, the message, in any way! "Thus saith the Lord" should be the final declaration in any matter. Biblical preaching must be rooted in Scripture.

Notice the place of the preached Word of God in Paul's theology. In Romans 10:13, he declares, "For everyone who calls on the name of the Lord shall be saved." Then, he proceeds to explain how this occurs. He argues, logically, that people cannot call on the Lord if they have not believed. And they cannot believe upon Him if they have no knowledge of Him. He then asks, "How can they hear without a preacher?" He then points out that preachers must be sent.[30]

His next line of reasoning is that not all who hear obey the gospel and confirms this truth, quoting Isaiah. He concludes, "So faith comes from what is heard, and what is heard comes through the message about Christ." Paul then addresses Israel's refusal to heed the message and observes, "All day long I have spread out hands to a disobedient and defiant people." [31]

Paul's point that I want to highlight is that grace comes through the preached Word. And it is the responsibility of the hearer to respond in faith. That said, the essence of preaching requires the proclamation of God's Word. Biblical preaching must be rooted in Scripture!

Third, biblical preaching is done by a spokesman who represents God. It is a dangerous and awesome experience when someone stands to preach as God's spokesman. It is dangerous and awesome for the preacher and carries weighty responsibilities. Recall James' somber warning, "Not many should become teachers [recall Eph. 4:11 and pastor-teacher], my brothers, knowing that we will receive a stricter judgment." [32] It is also dangerous and awesome for the hearer. The hearer, too, has great responsibility. In the modern quest for egalitarianism, we have lost, I fear, the healthy respect

---

30   Romans 10:14–15.
31   Romans 10:16–21.
32   James 3:1.

and deference to the authority of a God-called pastor-preacher proclaiming a message rooted in Scripture.

Scripture is replete with examples of men who were called to be God's spokesmen. Noah, according to 2 Peter 2:5, was a "preacher of righteousness." Moses argued with God when the Lord instructed him to return to Egypt as His spokesman. At Isaiah's Temple experience upon the occasion of Uzziah's death, the question is asked, "Who should I send? Who will go for Us?" And Isaiah responds, "Here I am. Send me." Jeremiah tells us, "If I say: I won't mention Him or speak any longer in His name, His message becomes a fire burning in my heart, shut up in my bones. I become tired of holding it in, and I cannot prevail."[33] Or consider Jonah, drafted by God to go and preach to the people of Ninevah. And recall Timothy to whom Paul exhorted, "Preach the Word!"

Our conclusion based upon the Word of God is that God calls men to preach His Word. Those whom He calls, He equips for the task. The most critical asset is that the God-called preacher is a man of faith expecting and anticipating God to move when the Word is preached.

Charles Spurgeon recounts the story of one of his students at the pastor's college, T. W. Medhurst. From his autobiography, Spurgeon writes:

> One day, with a very sad countenance, he said to me, "I have been preaching for three months, and I don't know of a single soul having been converted." Meaning to catch him by guile, and at the same time to teach him a lesson he would never forget, I asked, "So you expect the Lord to save souls every time you open your mouth?" "Oh, no, sir!" he replied. "Then," I said, "that is just the reason why you have not had conversions: 'According to your faith be it unto you.'[34]

Biblical preaching requires a spokesman who represents God. As God's spokesman, the preacher should always expect God to work through the preached Word!

Fourth, biblical preaching is, first, to believers. Here, it is for the purpose of communicating God's truth, reproof, correction, or training. It is for the purpose of edification. From 2 Timothy 3:16–17, Paul instructs the

---

33 Exodus 3:10, 18; 4:10–12; Isaiah. 6:8; Jeremiah. 20:9. Jonah 1:1–2, 2 Timothy 4:2.

34 *C.H. Spurgeon Autobiography* , Vol. 1, *The Early Years* (Edinburgh: The Banner of Truth Trust, reprinted 1981), 388.

younger preacher that the Word of God is His instrument to communicate His revealed truth (doctrine). It also points out when our lives are moving in a wrong direction (reproof), how to correct what is wrong (correction), and the disciplines needed to be trained in righteousness (training). These four benefits of Scripture affect aspirations, attitudes, behavior, beliefs, and values. As the Word of God is applied, the end result is that the man of God, which this writer believes can be applied to every believer, will be thoroughly equipped for every good work. Consider Jesus' words, "That they may see your good works and glorify your Father who is in Heaven." [35]

Fifth, biblical preaching is also to unbelievers. It has as its object either their conversion, or by default, their condemnation and judgment. Should they respond in faith to the preached word, it brings salvation. If they reject the appeal, it brings judgment. One of the major messages in the Old Testament prophets in that mercy spurned brings judgment.[36]

The dynamics of the salvation process are laid out clearly in Ephesians 2:8–10. It is initiated by grace. But grace requires our faith response. "By grace are you saved through faith." I believe the antecedent for "that" in "and that not of yourselves" refers to the salvation experience. Salvation is the gift. The end result of salvation is "good works." Hebrews 4:2 tells us, "The message heard did not benefit them, since they were not united with those who heard it by faith." The NIV translates this, "for we also have had the gospel preached to us, just as they did; but the message heard was of no value to them, because those who heard it did not combine it with faith." My point is that the failure to be saved is in the heart of the one who refuses to respond to God's grace by faith.

When the rich young ruler walked way from Jesus' invitation, it was not due to the dynamic of no effectual call, else Jesus is less than God. The rich young ruler's failure to come to Christ was in his own unwillingness. Is that not the same thing that Jesus said about the populace of Jerusalem in the days of His incarnation? He cried out, "Jerusalem, Jerusalem! The city that kills the prophets and stones those who are sent to her. How often I wanted to gather your children together, as a hen gathers her chicks under her wings, yet you were not willing!"[37]

If God commands all men everywhere to repent, will He not give grace for us to obey what He has commanded? Or should we actually believe

---

35   2 Timothy 3:16–17; Matthew 5:16
36   Matthew 6:10; Proverbs 14:34
37   Matthew 19:16–23; Luke 18:18–23; Matthew 23:37

that God invites but in reality He does not? My point is that when the preacher preaches the gospel, it is the obligation of the hearer to respond in repentance and faith. Otherwise, the listener is not accountable for his or her inability to respond! To hear the gospel preached and reject the salvation offered brings judgment and condemnation upon the hearer because he or she has rejected God's all-sufficient Savior. Biblical preaching to unbelievers is sufficient to bring them to salvation. [38]

Sixth, biblical preaching has as its ultimate intention to bring all hearers into Christian maturity and the culture into Christian conformity. Paul tells us in Romans that we are not to be conformed to this world, but to be transformed through the renewing of our minds. The same aspiration is found in Colossians when he writes, "That we may present every man complete in Christ." That is the goal for the individual![39]

I tell my students they have three targets as they preach. First, to unbelievers they preach evangelistic sermons to facilitate their salvation. To believers, they preach messages that edify. And to the culture, it is incumbent upon the preacher to address the great moral issues. This, I believe, is the essence of preaching the whole counsel of God. And this should be the goal of every biblical preacher!

---

38   Acts 17:30
39   Romans 12:2; Colossians 1:28

Chapter 5

Planning Ahead

Very few preachers have the skill set necessary for relying on what is commonly called a "Saturday-Night Special." That is, waiting until the last minute to put together one's thoughts with the end result that the weekly sermon(s) has both quality and freshness about it. In fact, I only know of one preacher who preached consistently superior messages while starting weekly from scratch. That was Charles Spurgeon.

Each Monday, Spurgeon would begin afresh his preparation for the coming Sunday's message. To our knowledge, he did not have a plan. Neither did he preach consecutively through books of the Bible, although he could have if his *Treasury of David* is any example of what he might have done.

Spurgeon often averaged eight to ten hours or more a day in study. He averaged reading a book a day. And he had a near-photographic memory. With that kind of giftedness and discipline, it was possible for him to wait until Saturday night to plan his outline for the next morning. Most of his sermons were expository, if you define it as preaching start to finish through a specific text of Scripture. As a rule, Spurgeon only carried a half-sheet of notes with him to the pulpit, primarily to jog his memory of the outline. He preached extemporaneously.

His *Autobiography* records a few occasions where, exhausted, he went to sleep on Saturday night without confirming his outline for the next day. On these occasions, his wife would hear him talk in his sleep and write down what he said. Either he outlined the sermon in his sleep or his wife could write some pretty effective outlines. Most preachers do not have the skill set or the spouse to follow this pattern of sermon preparation and produce consistently acceptable messages.

That being the case, it is incumbent for the preacher to work ahead in both the planning of his messages and in the capturing of ideas that will facilitate this process. Consider first how to find and formulate sermon ideas and second how to put these in a Planned Program of Preaching.

Sources of Sermon Ideas

If the preacher will discipline his thoughts and powers of observation, sermon ideas can be found in every direction. When I am preparing to address any group, I always ask three questions. To whom am I speaking? What are their needs? And what does God say? These questions help form a grid as I keep my eyes open for sermon ideas. Specifically, where do I look as I think about upcoming sermon series?

Before I go into detail of where to look, let me suggest that you do two things to help you capture ideas. I must confess that I have missed a lot of good ideas simply because I did not capture them at the moment. I am reminded of something my uncle, Ralph Toliver, once told me that he picked up as he served the Lord with the China Inland Mission. He related the old Chinese proverb, "The weakest ink is stronger than the strongest mind." That is, if you will write down a thought, you have captured it forever.

The first thing I suggest you do is purchase an inexpensive notebook. On the first page, simply put the year in which you are recording. Any time you have an idea, see an interesting phenomenon, observe a critical matter in the culture, or whatever, write it down. It may be an idea for a sermon or sermon series.

Second, keep a file folder in a handy place. I might be leafing through a magazine or newspaper and see something interesting. Tear it out and toss it in the file. Sometimes a card or an advertisement, any number of things that look interesting, can be collected. Simply throw it in the file (whether a file folder or an electronic file). The key is to capture it and have a system in place to retrieve it. When you begin to work on next year's sermon planning, pull out the notebook and the file. More than likely, you will have more ideas than you have days to preach. Then, all you have to do is prioritize the most important ideas and move full speed ahead.

With a mechanism in place to capture ideas, consider the following areas to look as sources of sermon ideas.

First, keep notes from your devotional reading. Every preacher knows the necessity of spending time daily in the Word. Any method is better than no method. Some read through the Bible once a year. Others read the same small book or chapters each day for a month. Others translate a passage out of their Hebrew Bible or Greek New Testament each day. I heard Billy Graham say once that he reads five Psalms and one Proverb daily. As you read the Word devotionally, the Holy Spirit will give you insights that you need and ought to record. These can be sources of sermon ideas.

Second, observe human need. Where are the people in your congregation hurting, and where do they need help? How about people in your community? What is on the front page of your newspaper? You will never run out of sermon ideas when you minister to people in their pain. Recall C. S. Lewis's observation that God shouts at us through our pain.

Third, observe cultural events and trends. Use these to connect with your congregation. Explain God's perspective on issues raised. When the movie *The DaVinci Code* came out, the premise of the movie was the humanity and nondivinity of Christ. Our worship team used this as a launching point to create a sermon series addressing the biblical foundation of our belief in the incarnation, the Trinity, and the essential doctrines of Christology. When moral issues are in the news, I will often attempt to provide a biblical perspective.

Fourth, capitalize on holidays, especially those with a religious significance. People expect to hear messages about the resurrection and its significance on Easter, gratitude before Thanksgiving, and typically a series leading up to Christmas. Most congregations want to honor service personnel on Veteran's Day and to have a patriotic emphasis on the Fourth of July weekend and Memorial Day weekend. Each nation has its special days, and wise preachers will capitalize on these days and not ignore them.

Fifth, when there is a crisis in the church or society, I would address the issues head on. When the country was attacked on September 11, 2001, wise preachers set aside what they had planned to preach and addressed the crisis. Your people want to know, "Does God have anything to say?" Your obligation is to give them that word from God.

Sixth, what are your church's goals for the year? These ought to be addressed. For many years, I would preach a "state of the church" address in January. If we had a major ministry emphasis or a building emphasis or a mission emphasis, these would be addressed in my sermons. We wanted our people to know "this is what we believe God wants us to do" and "here is how you fit in." An old cliché says, "What people are not up on, they are down on." Make sure your people are "up" on what is going on in the congregation. About the time you are sick of addressing an issue, some people will hear it for the very first time.

Seventh, good books, podcasts, CDs and DVDs that you have read or heard may be a great source for sermon material. I tell my students not to preach someone else's sermons. But if you gain insights from their work, use it. My friend, Adrian Rogers, used to say, "If my bullets fit your gun, fire away."

Another analogy says, "You can borrow some ingredients, but bake your own bread." Years ago, someone gave me a little book by Jack Hayford entitled, *How to Live Through a Bad Day.* This was a short book built off of his Easter Sunday message. It was actually a revisiting of Jesus' seven last words on the cross. It was a new approach to Russell B. Jones' classic *Gold from Golgotha.* I took Hayford's Easter sermon, isolated each of the seven sayings (points), and developed them into a series of messages that reached the pinnacle on Easter. I think we called the series, "How to Survive a Very Bad Day" and capitalized on the *Survivor* theme that was hot at the time.

Eighth, it is always wise to revisit the church's core values. These can easily be placed in sermons and sermon series. For example, on a regular basis I would address the lost in evangelistic messages. I also preached consistently on the church's priority of evangelism. Most church people, unless they are trained and challenged to the contrary, will have a "come to church as a spectator" mindset. We repeatedly emphasized the need for church members to share their faith. I also reminded them constantly that one of the most important things they could do is simply invite friends or family to worship with them. A statistic that surfaced a while back is that 85 percent of the lost and unchurched people in America would attend worship if someone would simply invite them. So, the core value of evangelism was reinforced from the pulpit.

Another core value is discipleship. Besides addressing the need for us to be disciples and make disciples, I would often preach a sermon series yearly on some aspect of discipleship and spiritual formation issues like personal Bible study, prayer, and other spiritual disciplines.

Worship is another core value. I preached messages on who we worship, what is worship, how do we worship, and why we worship. Worship does not come naturally. It is a behavior that must be taught and encouraged. I addressed this from the pulpit.

Fellowship is the next core value I addressed in my sermons. This subject focused on how to build relationships and minister in the congregation. I used to tell our folks that Sunday school (and our small group ministry) is the glue that holds us together. In the small groups, people know your name, pray for you, hurt with you, rejoice with you, and minister to you. Again, this must be modeled, taught, and caught. In fellowship, "love one another" is practiced best in the local congregation. As a core value, I would reinforce the need for fellowship in the church by demonstrating its priority in my messages.

Closely related to fellowship is the idea of community. This too is a core value. It focuses more specifically, however, on the concept that "you belong." When God calls us into His family and we respond by faith, we now belong to God's family, a new community. Because we belong, we now have a new identity. We want to reinforce this concept through the preaching of God's Word. When Paul, for example, became a follower of Jesus Christ, he became part of a new community with a new identity. The same is true for every new believer and new church member. Help your congregation to understand this.

Another core value is the emphasis we place on missions. We encourage our people to pray, give, and go. We highlight that God's will is that the entire world know Him, and that that will only happen as we take the gospel to a lost world. Each year we would have an emphasis on missions, and I would often preach a series to reinforce this core value.

Relationships and family are two additional core values. Seldom would a year pass that I did not have a sermon series on how to build relationships or preach on some dimension of family life. Some years I would do both. Recently, I preached a six-sermon series out of Proverbs on "What I Want My Kids to Know." Besides walking through the process of rearing children, I would emphasize the critical role parents play in assisting their children on this journey of growing up. My premise was that our goal as parents is to assist our children in their development from their absolute dependence upon us as parents to the place where they are absolutely dependent upon God.

I also emphasized the principle that every parent needs to give his or her children "roots and wings." Roots help them know who they are and that they belong. They give identity and security. When I talk about wings, I tell parents that their responsibility is to equip their children to become all God wants them to become and to give them permission and encouragement to pursue their dreams. Again, these are core values that must be emphasized through the preaching ministry of the church.

Another core value is stewardship. Building off the biblical principle that all we are and have belongs to God, then we are accountable for what we do with what we have been entrusted. This core value is greater than a yearly emphasis on tithing and giving. It mandates that all we are and have, our time, talents, treasure, relationships, and influence, everything must be managed in light of the fact that we are accountable to God for what we have and what we do with it.

The next core value is that we embrace a certain set of core beliefs that are delineated in our confessional documents. As a result, it is important that we periodically preach on the great doctrines of the faith. In most years, I would preach a doctrinal series.

A final core value that needs to be addressed from the pulpit is the critical issue of church health. Seldom would a year pass that I did not address this from either a single message or a series of messages. If the pastor does not address critical issues concerning the church's nature, how it is organized, how it functions, and the roles and responsibilities of leadership and members, disunity can easily infect the church. When Paul gave his Acts 20 address to the Ephesian elders, he warned them of enemies from without and within that will attack a congregation. Scripture tells us that Jesus came to destroy the works of the devil. It is obvious that Satan's design is to destroy the church. Wise pastors know the importance of preaching on the need for church health.

This is a representative sampling of sources for sermon ideas and a simple way to capture ideas. The next issue is once you have these ideas, what will you do with them? How do you turn ideas into a plan?

A Planned Program of Preaching

Each year, some time between Thanksgiving and the New Year, I would take a week to plan out next year's Planned Program of Preaching. When I was by myself, I would take my notebook and file folders where I have been collecting ideas, insights, and material over the previous year. Then I would write out the key ideas of what I believed our people needed to hear. Next, I would prioritize these as I prayed over them. "What do Your people need to hear, Lord?" was my prayer. Then I would think through the calendar. Is there a more appropriate time for me to address certain subjects? I would give our music team my sermon series, titles, and texts for January early in November. For music to meld with the message, musicians need lead time.

My approach to preaching took a bifocal approach. In the mornings, I would preach short series. In the evening, I would preach book by book and verse by verse. Only rarely did I deviate from this. One year I did preach a tandem series, morning and evening, that I called "The Alpha and Omega." In the mornings, I preached through Genesis, and in the evening, I preached through Revelation. Another year I preached a year-long series in the evening on "What We Believe." Here, I preached through our confessional statement, with the intention of helping our people grasp the great doctrines of our faith. For the most part, however, these were deviations from an established pattern.

When I began to plan my preaching for the coming year, I would follow a consistent set of steps. Step one was keeping a file folder and notebook where I recorded ideas. Step two was to prioritize the subjects I believed needed to be addressed. Step three entailed taking out a calendar for the next year. In this calendar, I would mark significant days, holidays, special events, and my own vacation days. With the focus on Sunday morning, I would look to see how many Sundays I would have for each series by breaking them on special days. I liked, for example, to start a new series on Easter. Often I would do a family series beginning on Mother's Day and concluding on Father's Day. Most years I would begin a Christmas series immediately after Thanksgiving and conclude Christmas weekend. I would plan my series on natural breaks.

If I were doing a series, for example, on prayer, and I realized that I had five Sundays to address this subject, I would think through my devotional reading and ask, where in Scripture is the discipline of prayer addressed clearly? I might select the Lord's Prayer from Matthew 6:1, 5–15; 7:7–11, or Luke 11 or John 17, or select one of Paul's prayers, or take a chapter out of the Psalms. Then, I would subdivide the text into five manageable sections of Scripture with the common thread of prayer while isolating the principal theme, the text, and key ideas.

If I selected the Matthew 6:1, 5–15; 7:7–11 passage, my series may look something like this:

1. Matthew 6:1, 5 — Why Are You Praying?
2. Matthew 6:6–8 — Who is Your Audience?
3. Matthew 6:9–13 — Ingredients of Meaningful Prayer
4. Matthew 6:14–15 — How Forgiveness and Prayer Connect
5. Matthew 7:7–11 — Promises You Can Claim

For a series title, I might select a descriptive approach like "Learning to Pray from the Son of God," or a more contemporary title like, "Connecting with God."

I suggest you plan your morning series before your evening series if you are in a congregation that has both. If your church is typical, you will have more church people and more lost people present on Sunday morning. You will have a more mature group in attendance on Sunday evening.

In step four, when I completed the number of series I would need in the morning and the number of times I would preach on Sunday evenings, I would enter these into my Planned Program of Preaching. In the Planned Program of Preaching, I would break the pages down by month. It is easiest to have separate calendars for morning and evening plans. On each page, I would identify the month, year, and service, whether morning or evening. I would have a place for the sermon series title. Next to each date, I would record the title, the text, and the theme. To the side, I would have a place for notes. At the bottom of the page, I would make notes of resources that I would want to use in preparation.

Step five would entail me giving this plan to my administrative assistant. She would type a final draft, and I would proof it. Once it was proofed, I would give a copy to our musicians so they could plan the music around the themes. Also, my assistant would make file folders for each sermon labeling the series, date, title, and text. I would have her photocopy pages out of reference books that I would use for textual study and background study. It was not unusual for each file folder to have eight to ten articles. Any notes that I had collected from the past year, I would place in the appropriate files. By doing this, when I began to work on next Sunday's messages, I would be light years ahead of the preacher who had to start from scratch.

Because our music staff and worship team had the sermon series ahead of time, we could work on ways to build the service around the theme. Over a series of decades, I developed this process that works for me as I planned my preaching. What I believe is critical is that you have a plan that works for you. This one worked for me … still does.

I find three advantages of having a Planned Program of Preaching. First, it helps the preacher ensure that the congregation will get a balanced spiritual diet. Preachers who do not have a plan tend to gravitate to their favorite subjects and may tend to emphasize one area at the expense of others. Being called to preach the whole counsel of God can be difficult if you are not evaluating whether or not your preaching emphasis is balanced.

Second, it keeps the preacher from functioning out of a reactionary mode. It is better to have a plan and to deviate from it on occasion than constantly to be preaching sermons based on what is happening this week. It also keeps the preacher from getting behind should the week be filled with unexpected interruptions.

And third, it gives the preacher more time to pray through and apply his messages to his congregation. If all the preacher's time is spent simply trying to decide what to preach, little time may be given to the vital issues of how this passage affects how we live.

Planning ahead is of infinite value to the preacher who wants to preach consistently effective biblical messages.

Chapter 6

A History of Preaching

When I did my doctoral work under Professor Scott Tatum, he delivered an introductory lecture on the value of studying the history of preaching. I have reflected on this for years. Here are my five reasons for studying the history of preaching.

First, we study the history of preaching because of its biblical significance. Early on, "thus saith the Lord" marked defining moments for the history of humanity. As Jesus trained His twelve, He sent them out preaching. At the church's birth, we are told that "Peter, taking his stand with the eleven, raised his voice and declared ..." When Paul mentored Timothy, he exhorted him to "preach the Word!"[40] Preaching was the priority ministry in Scripture.

Second, we study the history of preaching because of its historic significance. In various times and places, preaching was used by God to bring changes to cultures, societies, denominations, churches, and individuals. How different Great Britain would have been if John Wesley and George Whitefield had not preached, and they did!

Third, we study the history of preaching for its practical and professional significance. We understand how great preachers have preached in the past by studying their sermons and their lives. We learn insights into the dynamics of preaching. We see right and wrong ways of preaching and thereby learn from those who have gone before us.

---

40   Genesis 22:16; Exodus 4:22; Luke 9:1–2, 11; Acts 2:14; 2 Timothy 4:1–2

Fourth, we study the history of preaching because of its personal significance. We read and listen to great preachers in order to learn their ways. How did they prepare themselves? How did they prepare their messages? How did they approach the Scripture? How did they illustrate and apply their messages? As we study great preachers, we allow their strengths to strengthen us. We are personally sharpened by studying history's greats.

And fifth, we study the history of preaching because of its spiritual significance. Just as the preached Word ministered to people in its contemporary setting, it still ministers as we read and listen to it again. Who has not been moved by Latimer's "Sermon on the Plough" or Tennent's "The Danger of an Unconverted Ministry"?

Here, then, are five reasons to study the history of preaching. If we study these men and their messages, we will become better preachers. We become better partly by studying the best. Now, consider the role of preaching in history.

Preaching in the Bible

The first preacher in Scripture is God Himself. Repeatedly, in the early chapters of Genesis is the statement, "And God said." In Genesis 2:16, we read, "And the Lord God commanded the man ..." In the Old Testament, we read the sermons of Moses. Deuteronomy begins, "These are the words Moses spoke to all Israel ..." The Hebrew prophets are prototypes for the preacher today.

In the Gospels, Jesus' forerunner, John the Baptist, came preaching repentance and pointing men to Jesus. Jesus Himself came preaching. He trained His twelve and sent them out to preach. In His eschatological address, Jesus declared, "And this gospel of the kingdom shall be preached in the whole world for a witness to all the nations, and then the end shall come."[41]

The book of Acts is filled with preaching. The church was born with the coming of the Holy Spirit and the preaching of the Word. At the preaching of Peter, the crowd cried out, "Brethren, what shall we do?" When the need for additional workers was evident, the apostles declared, "We will devote ourselves to prayer, and to the ministry of the Word." When the Jerusalem persecution became unbearable, Acts tells us that the early believers "were scattered" and that "those who had been scattered

---

41   Matthew 3:1–2, 4:17, 23; 9:35; 24:14; John 1:29; Luke 9:2, 6

went about preaching the Word." Acts 17 records for us the sermon Paul preached to the Athenians, declaring, "What therefore you worship in ignorance, this I proclaim unto you."[42]

From the outset, preaching was the priority ministry of the church.

The Patristic Era

Preaching played a critical role in the growth and development of Christianity during the Patristic era. Although records are scarce, we do have some knowledge of preaching during these post-Apostolic times. Of course, persecution limited the amount of time and energy that could be given to recording the preaching during these early years. Also, during the initial years of the Patristic era, we find an extreme distrust of the Christian community toward pagan learning and classical rhetoric. The records tell us that the earliest preaching was saturated with Scripture and early on we read of the "homily," a running commentary on the text of Scripture as the normative pattern in preaching. [43]

The Apostolic Fathers wrote from approximately AD 70 to 160. Polycarp, Ignatius, and Clement of Rome played prominent roles. The oldest surviving sermon manuscript is Clement's Second Letter to the Corinthians.

The Apologists came into prominence from around AD 120 to 200. These men wrote to dispel the multitude of false accusations made against Christianity. These, represented by scholars like Justin Martyr and Tertullian, were significant because of their interaction of Christian beliefs with the learning and philosophy of the pagan world.

The Ante-Nicene Theologians wrote from AD 180 until 300. Prominent among these men are Clement of Alexandria, Origen, Gregory of Thaumaturgus, Irenaeus, Tertullian (he bridges the Apologists and the Ante-Nicene Theologians), and Cyprian. From the perspective of preaching, Origen is the more important representative. Although his name is most associated with the allegorical school of hermeneutics, he did maintain two principles that were significant to the study of preaching. First, he laid great stress on the need for precise exegesis in the historical and grammatical preparation of the sermon. Also, he developed a form for

---

42 Acts 2:37; 6:4; 8:1, 4; 17:23.

43 The Epistle of Ignatius to Polycarp 5:1 in *The Early Church Fathers*, Vol. 1 in the Christian Classics series (Nashville: Broadman & Holman, 1979), 87; O.C. Edwards, *A History of Preaching* (Nashville: Abingdon Press, 2004), 14–16.

the simple exposition of Scripture. He was the first to insist on the need to preach upon a single passage of Scripture. [44]

Dargan summarized the preaching of the earlier Patristic period as being obscure but significant. He assessed the preaching of this era thusly:

1. It was convinced of the truth of the Gospels
2. It preached lofty morality
3. It was firmly based on the authority of Scripture
4. While not explicit in doctrine, it contained the great teachings of Christianity [45]

From 300 to 430, we discover one of the climactic periods of Christian development. During this period, Christianity was first tolerated and then embraced by the empire. Schools were opened to Christians, the Canon was settled, and doctrine was stabilized. Prominent preachers in the Greek-speaking east were Athanasius, Basil, Gregory of Nyssa, Gregory of Nazianzus, and John Chrysostom. Prominent in the Latin-speaking west were Cyprian, Hilary, Ambrose, and Augustine. Of these late Patristic preachers, Chrysostom, Ambrose, and Augustine stand out.

Preaching advancements in this Post-Nicene era saw the building of churches that became preaching centers, special days of preaching, and a restriction of preaching to bishops and presbyters. Sermons in this era contained more doctrine and more illustrations than the previous times. Greek rhetoric began to influence pulpit style.

Many consider John Chrysostom (347–407) to be the greatest preacher in Christian history. His name means "golden-mouth." A student of rhetoric under Libanius, Chrysostom was also a trained attorney. He entered monastic life in 374, was ordained a deacon in 381, and was ordained a priest in 386. He began to preach in Antioch at the age of thirty-nine. His preaching style was simple and direct. He preached tirelessly on the moral issues of his day. In 397, he was literally kidnapped and taken to preach in Constantinople, from which he was ultimately banished because of his preaching against Empress Eudoxia's love of pleasure. He died in exile in 407.[46]

---

44   Clyde E. Fant, Jr. and William M. Pinson, Jr., *20 Centuries of Great Preaching*. Volume One. (Dallas: Word Books, 1971), 36.
45   Edwin C. Dargan, *A History of Preaching*, Volume I (Grand Rapids: Baker Books, 1954), 59–60.
46   Fant and Pinson, I: 53–69

He was known principally for following the Antiochan (literal) school of hermeneutics, embracing the historical-grammatical approach to interpretation.

Chrysostom's sermons are still understandable today. Although he did not indulge in allegory, he would slip into typology at times. His primary style was the homily. His great strength was in making the Bible text simple, its application unmistakable, and illustrations memorable. His hearers remarked about his ability to move his listeners through his delivery. He started slowly but then accelerated his pace as he moved into his sermon. His extant sermons number over one thousand. [47]

In the west, Ambrose and Augustine merit special attention. Ambrose is most well-known for his influence upon Augustine. Ambrose was the governor in Milan. Through an interesting set of circumstances, he was drafted to become bishop of Milan in 374. In a span of eight days, he was baptized, gave away his wealth, and was consecrated as bishop. Dunn-Wilson remarks, "The weight of history is that he was an outstanding preacher and teacher." Coupled with that is the fact that he was a great teacher of preachers. [48]

No doubt, Augustine is proof of Ambrose's persuasive qualities. The young student of rhetoric who went to hear how Ambrose spoke was soon persuaded of what he spoke. Most historians consider Augustine the greatest Christian leader between Paul and Luther. From the perspective of preaching, Augustine's principal work is *On Christian Doctrine*, a treatise on preaching. Besides leaving behind almost seven hundred manuscripts, it is estimated that Augustine preached almost eight thousand sermons in his lifetime. As mentioned earlier, Augustine was trained in classical rhetoric, was heavily influenced by Aristotle and Cicero, and emphasized the place of ethos, pathos, and logos in preaching.

With Augustine's death in AD 430, the Patristic era comes to a close and the Medieval Era begins.

The Medieval Era

The medieval era can be subdivided into three parts: the Dark Age (430–1054), the Scholastic Age (1054–1361), and the Age of the Pre-Reformers (1361–1517).

---

47   Stott, *Between*, 20–21; Fant and Pinson, I: 53–69.
48   David Dunn-Wilson, *A Mirror for the Church* (Grand Rapids: Eerdmans Press, 2005), 88.

The Dark Age was characterized by the dissolution of the Roman Empire, barbarian invaders, the rise of European powers, the emergence of Islam, and conflict between the eastern and western churches. Poverty was rampant.

Preaching during the Dark Age was marked by decline, the rise of liturgy, and morally and intellectually weak clergy. The churches had an over-emphasis on Mary and the sacraments and an under-emphasis on the Scriptures. The principal form of preaching remained the homily. The most prominent preacher during this period is Boniface (680–755).

The Scholastic Age saw a growing power struggle between the monarchies and the papacy. The middle class emerged, and there was an expansion of commerce. This time period saw the rise of the universities and intellectual pursuits. It also saw the growth of mysticism, larger crowds attending services with preaching, and sermons that depended too much on allegory and too little on Scripture.

During the Scholastic Age, we see three distinct types of preaching: scholastic represented by Thomas Aquinas, popular demonstrated by Francis and Dominic, and mystical, whose strongest representative was John Tauler. During this era, we saw an exponential rise in the number of books produced as pulpit helps.

Bernard of Clairvaux (1091–1153) was known as an outstanding preacher. He was so influential that when he decided to join the Cistercian Order, twenty-nine other men joined with him. As a preacher, he was instrumental in birthing the second crusade. In his preaching style, he was a curious mixture of popular, scholastic, and mystic. His preaching focused on two items: to defend the church from heresy and to enlist men for the second crusade. His theological system viewed preaching as the principal means of grace. [49]

Francis of Assisi founded the Franciscan Order in 1209. He was famous for saying, "Unless you preach everywhere you go, there is no need to go anywhere to preach."[50]

Dominic, a contemporary of Francis, founded the Dominican Order as an Order of Preachers. Whereas Francis did not emphasize education and preparation, Dominic insisted on it. Three years after Dominic's death, Humbert de Romans entered the Dominican Order. In 1254, he became the master general of the Dominicans. Humbert was famous for not only being a great preacher but also for being a great teacher of

49 Fant and Pinson, I: 143–8.
50 Ibid., I: 169–79.

preachers. The Franciscans and Dominicans were known primarily as popular preachers.

The greatest scholastic preacher was Thomas Aquinas. He chose to affiliate with the Dominicans because of their insistence on preaching and academics. Aquinas' approach to preaching was to use the best of Greek philosophy to argue the case for the Christian faith. Most of his extant sermons are briefs, logical in development, and homilies in format. It is said that when Aquinas preached that men were moved to tears. He was known for his intensity in the pulpit. At times, he did revert to allegory.

John Tauler (1290–1361) is the classic mystic preacher. Like Aquinas, he too affiliated with the Dominicans. His emphasis was on the soul's union with God. Interestingly, most of his preaching was to nuns. Like those of his era, he relied heavily on allegory but in his application excoriated those who trusted in good works as a means of salvation. We should note that Luther studied his sermons and was influenced by them.

The later portion of the Medieval Era may be considered the Age of the Pre-Reformers. Essentially, these preachers prepared the way for the Reformation. In fact, Franciscan leader Bernardino of Siena (1380–1444) stated that if a choice had to be made between the Mass and the sermon, the priest should give attention to the latter. This helped set the stage for the exaltation of not only preaching, but also the Scripture as superior to the traditions of the church.

In the Pre-Reformation era, four developments paved the way for the Reformation. The Renaissance provided a renewed interest in the ancient languages. Gutenburg's printing press (1456) made widespread dissemination of written materials possible. The spirit of nationalism allowed nation-states to break emotionally with Rome. And the corruption of the papacy with two, then three, popes simultaneously caused the common man to question papal authority.

Humanly speaking, four Pre-Reformers prepared the way for the Protestant Reformation. These were John Wycliffe of England, John Huss of Bohemia (the present Czech Republic), Giralamo Savonarola of Italy, and Desiderius Erasmus of Rotterdam.

John Wycliffe (1324/1330–1384) was known as the "Morning star of the Reformation." From a well-to-do family, he attended Oxford University. By 1370, he was Oxford's premier philosopher and theologian. He was also preoccupied with training preachers. These "Lollards" were sent out across the countryside to preach the Scriptures. In his work, he was highly critical of the Roman Catholic system and exalted Scripture as the norm for

Christianity's faith and practice. Wycliffe preached two types of sermons. Latin sermons were for the academic community. English sermons were for the common man. Most of his sermons followed the homily style, and he was not so far removed from his cultural setting that he completely discarded the use of allegory.

Wycliffe's contribution to preaching was primarily his insistence on preaching the naked text. Sermons, he taught, should be based upon Scripture alone. He also promoted preaching in the vernacular. Perhaps his greatest influence was upon John Huss. Although Wycliffe died of a stroke, after his death, the Roman Catholic authorities dug up his corpse, burned it, and scatter his ashes to the wind.

John Huss (1372–1415), who was greatly influenced by the writings of Wycliffe, studied at the University of Prague. He preached against Roman Catholic doctrine and for biblical Christianity. He was condemned and burned at the stake at the Council of Constance in 1415.

In Florence, Italy, Giralamo Savonarola (1452–1498) initiated a reform movement. He was known as a gifted orator, social reformer, and in time a martyr. For the most part, he was a prophetic preacher with a three-fold emphasis: the church will be severely punished, the church will be renewed, and all of this will transpire quickly.

Desiderius Erasmus (1468–1536) is one of the greatest scholars of the Renaissance and Reformation. A tireless critic of the Roman Catholic Church, Erasmus is noticed for his scathing critique, *The Praise of Folly*. His most enduring work is his Greek New Testament. Although he prepared the way for the Reformation, he refused to join it. The assessment of history is that Erasmus laid the egg that Luther hatched.

Many are unaware that Erasmus's last work, *Ecclesiastes*, was a treatise on preaching. Heavily influenced by Augustine, Erasmus emphasizes the importance of biblical character, displays an influence by Cicero and Quintilian, and provides advice on how to effectively communicate. Edwards notes that this work represents the great watershed in the history of Christian rhetoric influencing both Catholic and Protestant preaching.[51]

The Reformation Era (1517–1572)

In the Reformation era, preaching replaces the Mass as the centerpiece of worship. The principle of *sola scriptura* emerges so that Scripture provides the ultimate and final authority. During the Reformation, we see a new

---

51   Edwards, 274–79.

emphasis on grace and faith. Sermons are built upon exegesis and are an exposition of Scripture. The Reformation is an age of great preaching and great preachers.

Martin Luther (1483–1546), an Augustinian monk who was converted in his "tower experience," provided the philosophical, theological, and personal framework to launch the Reformation as he nailed his Ninety-Five Theses to the church house door at Wittenburg on October 31, 1517.

Luther, although a great theologian and reformer, always considered his first responsibility to be preaching. "Luther's expositions in preaching varied from greatly detailed studies to highly generalized essays, but seldom did he strain the meaning of a passage or indulge in allegory." Luther worked diligently to make his sermons simple and clear. Rarely containing a definite introduction or conclusion, Luther believed the body of the sermon was the only important part. As a result, most of Luther's sermons followed a simply homily. [52]

Consider Luther's advice to preachers: "These are the three things, it is commonly said, that mark a good preacher; first, that he take his place; secondly, that he open his mouth and say something; thirdly that he know when to stop." [53] Luther left over twenty-three hundred sermons.

In Zurich, Switzerland, the Reformation was led by Ulrich Zwingli. By 1525, the city had fully embraced the Reformation. Although Zwingli preached almost daily, few of his sermons remain because he had no scribes to record them as did Luther and Calvin. Zwingli's normative approach was to preach without notes. His sermons fall essentially into two categories. He primarily preached verse by verse through books. On occasion, however, he would pull away and preach on a predetermined theme. For Zwingli, Scripture dominates tradition. Zwingli, according to eyewitnesses, had poor delivery, yet his content led to his domination of Zurich. As with Luther, preaching spearheaded the Reformation.

The great second generation reformer is John Calvin (1509–1564). As a preacher, Calvin was thoroughly committed to the exposition of Scripture, and that, verse by verse. In the pulpit, he spoke without notes and often without specific preparation. It is said of Calvin that he spoke deliberately, slowly, and directly. Although his sermons lacked humor, they did not lack human interest. His sermons were colorful and reflected a variety of

---

52   Fant and Pinson, II: 10.

53   Hugh Kerr, *A Compend of Luther's Theology* (Philadelphia: Westminster Press, 1966), 150.

illustrations from the life of Geneva. Because Calvin had scribes to assist him, over two thousand manuscripts remain of his sermons.[54]

The Anabaptist (free church) movement was actually born when the Swiss Brethren separated from Zwingli in Zurich in 1525. George Blaurock, Conrad Grebel, Felix Manz, and Michael Sattler were each great preachers in their own right. The greatest and most articulate preacher among the Anabaptists was Balthazar Hubmaier (1485?–1528). William Estep points out that in one year alone, over six thousand baptisms were conducted under Hubmaier's ministry. According to Dargan, "All accounts agree that Hubmaier was a forcible and eloquent preacher." Bullinger and others state that the "results of his work in every place where he served as pastor show that he had unusual power of influencing men to action by his preaching." Most Anabaptist scholars agree that Hubmaier was their greatest preacher. Sadly, none of his sermons remain.[55]

The greatest preacher in the Dutch Reformation was James Arminius (1560–1609). Trained in Reformed Theology, he broke with his Geneva professors over their understanding of soteriology. Arminius was a brilliant scholar and sound theologian. In 1591, Arminius began to preach through Romans. His crisis came when he reached Romans 7:14. This began a debate that eventually left Arminius as an outsider to his Reformed brethren. His epitaph read thusly: "Subtle in intellect, and great in speech ..."[56]

In Great Britain, two preachers stood out above the others during the Reformation: Hugh Latimer (1490–1555) and John Knox (1513–1572). Latimer is clearly the greatest preacher of the Anglican Reformation. At Cambridge, Latimer embraced Reformation doctrine and here began to preach. One who heard his early sermons stated, "None except the stiff-necked and uncircumcised in heart went away from his preaching without being affected with high detestation of sin and moved unto all godliness and virtue."[57]

As a preacher, Latimer spoke without notes. It is fortunate that scribes recorded many of his sermons. Dargan, commenting on Latimer's sermons, said:

> They bear in many traits, both of thought and style, the
> stamp of a marked individuality. Courage combined with

---

54 Fant and Pinson, II: 144.

55 William R. Estep, *The Anabaptist Story* (Grand Rapids: William B. Eerdmans Publ., 1963), 64; Dargan, I: 471.

56 Mendal Taylor, *Exploring Evangelism* (Kansas City: Nazarene Publishing House, 1964), 203.

57 Dargan, I: 488.

shrewdness and tact, strong convictions and deep feelings joined to a lively wit and quaint humor, clear and firm grasp of truth along with an easy familiarity of manner, indifference to exact analysis and division, yet an orderly presentation and vigorous movement of thought, are some of the things which show themselves to the reader of his sermons.[58]

His sermons are not so much exposition as application. Nevertheless, Latimer has a high regard for the absolute authority of Scripture. Speaking to a friend, he said, "I am resolved to be guided only by the Book of God, and sooner than depart one jot from that, let me be trampled under the feet of wild horses." Herein lies the secret of Latimer's greatness. Most agree that his greatest sermon was "The Sermon on the Plough."[59]

John Knox, the fiery reformer of Scotland, combined preaching and political revolution in such a way that Scotland underwent the most thorough reformation of any nation in Europe. Fewer of Knox's sermons remain than for any other major magisterial reformer—only two. All accounts confirm that he was clear, forceful, and bold in his delivery. From the little evidence remaining, it appears that Knox's sermons were clear in organization and that he had an affinity for biblical illustrations. Commenting upon the impact of Knox's sermons, James Melville, who often heard him, related, "In the opening up of his text he was moderate to the space of half an hour; but when he entered to application, he made me so thrill and tremble, I could not hold a pen to write." No doubt the greatest quality Knox brought to the pulpit was his courage in the face of opposition and adversity. [60]

The Puritans and Pietists

The term *Puritan* was originally one of derision. It did, however, identify those who wanted to purify the church. Ironwy Morgan said they are best identified as "the Godly preachers."[61]

Puritan preaching was most well known for five elements. First, it was saturated with Scripture. Second, it was unashamedly doctrinal. Third, everything about the message was practical. Fourth, it focused

---

58 Ibid., I: 493–94.

59 J.H. Merle d'Aubigne, *The Reformation of England*, 2 vols. (London: Banner of Truth, reprinted 1962), II: 387; Stott, 26–28

60 Fant and Pinson, II: 185, 195.

61 Stott, 28

on the complete conversion of each listener. And finally, it was intensely symmetrical. Martyn Lloyd-Jones notes that for the Puritans, preaching was central. Often sermons were delivered extemporaneously. Puritans insisted that the sermon took priority over sacraments and ceremonies. For the most part, Puritans were well educated. [62]

Three of the most prominent textbooks on preaching during this era were William Perkins' *The Art of Prophesying*, William Ames' *The Marrow of Sacred Divinity*, and Richard Bernard's *The Faithful Shepherd*. These texts maintained that sermons should be comprised of four elements. First was the explication of the text. Second was the derivation of the doctrine. Third was the development of reasons for the doctrine. And finally, the "use" or application concluded the message.

Famous Puritan preachers were Richard Sibbes, Richard Baxter, and John Bunyan. Of course, there were hundreds of good and godly preachers among the Puritans, but these stand out.

In post-Reformation Lutheran thought, a rigid orthodoxy quickly set in. John Arndt reacted to this reality and wrote *True Christianity,* in which he argued that "true Christianity consists, not in words or in external show, but in living faith from which arise righteous fruits, and all manner of Christian virtues, as from Christ himself." [63]

Heavily influenced by Arndt was Philip Jacob Spener, known as the father of Pietism. When he was invited to write the foreword for a collection of sermons by Arndt, Spener produced a masterful essay, *Pia Desideria,* in 1675. After the second printing of the sermons, the sermons were dropped and the essay, a short book, took on a life of its own. This seminal work of Pietism was essentially a game plan for the church's renewal. Part of the renewal effort prescribed by Spener was a renewed emphasis on preaching. Spencer argues forcefully, "Preaching should be the divine means to save the people, and so it is proper that everything be directed to that end." To Spener, the principal issue with respect to preaching is this: "Our whole Christian religion consists of the inner man or the new man, whose soul is faith and whose expressions are the fruits of life, and all sermons should be aimed at this." [64]

---

62 Joel R. Beeke, *Puritan Evangelism: A Biblical Approach* (Grand Rapids: Reformation Heritage Books, 2007), 9–48.

63 *Pietism* in the Christian Classics series (Nashville: B&H, 2007), 9–48.

64 Philip Jacob Spener, *Pia Desideria,* Theodore G. Tappert, trans. and ed, (Philadelphia: Fortress Press, reprinted 1964), 116; Edwards, 840–66.

Spener's heir apparent was August Hermann Francke. Like Spener, he was known for his strong preaching, his promotion of foreign missions, and his attention to pietistic principles. Francke, however, was more of an activist than Spener. His work at the University of Halle helped turn Pietism into a movement. In his own writings on preaching, Francke insisted that its purpose was to bring sinners to Christ. [65]

The third principal leader of the Pietist movement was Count Nicholas von Zinzendorf. He eventually founded Herrnhut, "The Lord's Watch," and from this vantage point sent out preachers around the world. Eventually, Moravians who emerged out of Herrnhut would have a significant influence on John Wesley and the Evangelical Awakening in Great Britain.

The Evangelical Awakening and the First Great Awakening

The Evangelical Awakening in Great Britain and the First Great Awakening in America were two manifestations of the same event. In Great Britain, the Awakening was so strong that the course and character of the nation was changed. Historians credit John Wesley and his movement for preventing the bloodbath of the French Revolution from coming to the British Isles. The principal leaders of the Evangelical Awakening were John and Charles Wesley and George Whitefield.

While students at Oxford University, the three comprised the core of the "Holy Club," a student organization focused on small group discipleship and outreach. With all of their disciplines, John was outwardly successful but inwardly still empty.

In 1735, both the Wesleys departed for the Americas to serve as missionaries. On the trip over, both were influenced by the piety of the Moravians who were their traveling companions. In Georgia, John particularly considered himself an abject failure. In his journal, he wrote, "I went to America to convert the Indians; but Oh! Who shall convert me?" He returned to England depressed and discouraged.[66]

On May 4, 1738, John Wesley attended a worship service conducted by Peter Bohler, a Moravian preacher. Concerning the meeting, John noted, "I felt my heart strangely warmed," and attributes this moment as his conversion. The following year, Wesley joined Whitefield in open-air preaching in Bristol. Wesley continued open-air preaching the rest of his life.

---

65   Ibid.
66   Fant and Pinson, II: 5.

In his lifetime, it is estimated that Wesley at times preached to over twenty thousand people, averaged traveling twenty thousand miles a year on horseback (two hundred fifty thousand miles in his lifetime), and preached more than forty-two thousand sermons. He also penned over two hundred works. In summary, his preaching was biblical, focused on the love of God, and often was a running homily on his text or his theme. He always preached for a verdict.

George Whitefield, in contrast to the Wesleys, did not come from a Christian home. Early in his life, he displayed gifts for drama and rhetoric. When he had the opportunity to attend Oxford, he affiliated with the Holy Club, became fast friends with the Wesleys, and immediately began to engage in evangelistic preaching. Whitefield had a compulsive preoccupation to lead people to Christ. Because many churches were closed to him due to his passionate preaching, he went to the fields and preached to the masses. This became the pattern of his ministry.

In his lifetime, Whitefield preached in both Great Britain and the Americas. He crossed the Atlantic thirteen times. He preached over eighteen thousand sermons. His preaching was filled with emotion. He did not use manuscripts. His mannerisms were vigorous. He often used humor. He was known as a clear biblical preacher. Like Wesley, he always preached for a verdict. Particularly in the Americas, Whitefield is considered to be the one personality who tied the First Great Awakening in it regional manifestations into one massive movement.

The First Great Awakening in the Americas saw over one hundred fifty thousand conversions. Coupled with this was the planting of hundreds of churches. In the Middle Colonies, Theodore Frelinghuysen, a Dutch Reformed pastor, was considered the beginner of the great work. He was heavily influenced by the Pietists. His good friend was Gilbert Tennent, a Presbyterian pastor. Tennent was known for his sermon, "The Danger of an Unconverted Ministry." In New England, the great leader was Jonathan Edwards in Northampton, Massachusetts, where he pastored the Congregational Church. In 1740, he preached his famous, "Sinners in the Hands of an Angry God." In the southern colonies, outstanding leaders were the Methodist Devereux Jarratt and the Baptist work at Sandy Creek under the leadership of Dan Marshall and Shubal Stearns.

Consider Jonathan Edwards as an example of the preaching in the First Great Awakening. As a preacher, he followed the classic model established by William Perkins. Edwards left over twelve hundred sermon notes and manuscripts. For the most part, he was expositional in his approach. His hermeneutic model was to see everything through a Christological lens. He used illustrations sparingly, but when he did, they were sourced either from Scripture or from the world of nature. As he preached, he was heavy on application. His principal approach to sermon organization was: 1. An expansion of the text; 2. An outline of the doctrine in logical order; 3. The application. His sermons were often an hour or more in length. He was so articulate that his hearers said that he could paint pictures with words. Not surprisingly, he often studied twelve to fourteen hours a day.

The spiritual intensity of the First Great Awakening waned in time. The Revolutionary War exacerbated the spiritual decline. Coupled with the affects of the war was the growing influence of atheism and deism from men like Thomas Paine.

The Second Great Awakening

In 1794, Isaac Backus and Stephen Gano, plus a score of other religious leaders, issued a "Concert of Prayer" in response to the declining spirituality in America. The circular letter invited pastors and churches to band together with them in prayer for spiritual awakening.

When the Second Great Awakening came to the Americas, it came first in the east, primarily in the colleges. Lyman Beecher, who was a student at Yale in 1795, described it thusly: "The college was in a most ungodly state. The college church was almost extinct." A poll at Harvard revealed not one believer in the entire student body. Princeton found only two believers. [67]

The best known of the college revivals is the story of Yale. In 1795, Timothy Dwight, grandson of Jonathan Edwards, ascended to the presidency upon the death of Ezra Stiles. About his new responsibility Dwight wrote, "To build up a ruined college is a difficult task." Dwight confronted the infidelity head on. In 1802, half the student body came to faith in Christ.[68]

With respect to preaching, Dwight studied long hours with great intensity and preached extemporaneously. As a rule, he carried a brief outline to the pulpit with him. He spoke rapidly, with few gestures. In his later years, it was common for Dwight to dictate his sermons for publication. He appealed both to logic and emotion in his messages. He

---

67 William Warren Sweet, *Religion in America* (Grand Rapids: Baker Book House, 1979), 223–224; J. Edwin Orr, Dallas Prayer Conference transcript, "The Role of Prayer in Spiritual Awakening) n.d.

68 Keith J. Hardman, *The Spiritual Awakeners* (Chicago: Moody Press, 1983), 122.

is credited for being the most important preacher of the Second Great Awakening. Of special note is the fact that he mentored the next generation of preachers like Lyman Beecher.

Whereas the eastern phase of the Second Great Awakening was not overly emotional, the western phase stood in stark contrast. Outstanding preachers in the frontier of Kentucky were Peter Cartwright, James McGready, Barton Stone, and Alexander Campbell. The climax of the western phase was the great Cane Ridge Camp Meeting in August 1801. Preaching was loud, intense, emotional, and Christ-centered.

The Nineteenth Century

For the sake of brevity, we will restrict our review of the nineteenth century to Great Britain and America. The greatest preacher in the first third of the nineteenth century was Thomas Chalmers of Scotland. It was said of Chalmers that he once had to climb through a window to get to the pulpit, the crowd was so large.

As a preacher, his flow was eloquent. He was noted for his descriptive powers. He made full use of imagination. His diction reflected a rugged Scotsman. Often his sermons contained only one or two points. He drove home his principal theme with great repetition. More importantly, he was known for his clarity. Repetition and illustration helped make his sermons clear. Although he preached from a manuscript written in his own shorthand, he was known for his vigorous gestures. One criticism that may be valid was that often his sentences were too long. His most famous sermon was "The Expulsive Power of a New Affection."[69]

Close behind Chalmers was Robert Murray McCheyne, whose life tragically was cut short by illness. Although his preaching ministry covered only seven years, he is still considered one of history's best preachers. One of his greatest sermons was "The Vision of Dry Bones." As to style, McCheyne wrote out his sermons but preached without notes. He was known for his deep piety.[70]

The middle of the nineteenth century saw the rise of numerous great preachers in Britain. Thomas Guthrie, F. W. Robertson, and William Chalmers Burns stand out. The final third of the century saw preachers like H. P. Liddon, Alexander Maclaren, R. W. Dale, and Joseph Parker. Yet none excelled Charles Spurgeon, who was known as the "Prince of Preachers."

---

69   Fant and Pinson, III: 259–67.
70   Ibid., IV: 261–70.

Charles Hadden Spurgeon (1834–1892) served as pastor of the Metropolitan Tabernacle in London for over thirty years. In that period, his church had over ten thousand baptisms. Spurgeon was known for his great pulpit ability. For the most part, Spurgeon was an expositor of his text. He believed in the absolute inerrancy of the Scripture. His sermon was often a thematic treatment of the text. On occasion he would "spiritualize" his text, which was his term for allegorizing. For example, he likened the church to Noah's Ark and the one door as the one way of salvation. He was a master in his use of illustration and application.

Spurgeon normally took a brief outline of his sermon with him to the pulpit. He preached extemporaneously. He customarily had his sermons recorded by a stenographer, and then he edited them for publication on Monday. Those who assess his pulpit ministry have concluded that Spurgeon was much more concerned to prepare himself than his message before he preached. His delivery was often in a conversational tone, and during the message he demonstrated a profound earnestness that his hearers might respond.

Every preacher would benefit from reading Spurgeon's *Lectures to My Students* and *An All Round Ministry*. These works have inspired many preachers for generations.

In the States, the preaching of Charles Finney and D. L. Moody stand out. Finney (1792-1875) was trained as an attorney and always approached his preaching as one preaching for a verdict. He was known to be pietistic in his personal life. He spent long hours in prayer. When he preached, he called for decisions. It was said of Finney that he was crude, blunt, passionate, and extravagant. Besides being an outstanding evangelist, he was also a moral crusader.

D. L. Moody (1837–1899) began his evangelistic career in 1871 after having been a successful shoe salesman. Together with Ira Sankey, he conducted preaching campaigns in Great Britain and America. He established three Bible institutes. His preaching focused primarily on the love of God, the danger of hell, and the immediate need of surrendering to Jesus Christ. His strength was in his ability to illustrate in story and make emotional application.

Another outstanding preacher of the nineteenth century was Phillips Brooks (1835–1893). He coined the definition of preaching as the "communication of truth by man to men" or as truth through personality. He delivered the Lyman Beecher lectures at Yale in 1877.

Space will not permit a detailed review of other nineteenth-century standouts like Sam Jones, John Jasper, Henry Ward Beecher, Lyman Beecher, T. Dewitt Talmage, and Walter Rauschenbush. Perhaps, though, it would be wise to recognize John A. Broadus, professor of homiletics at Southern Seminary. His text, *On the Preparation and Delivery of Sermons*, has been a classic for over one hundred years.

Preaching in the Twentieth Century

When Michael Duduit served as editor of *Preaching Magazine*, he coordinated an effort to identify the century's ten greatest preachers. Not making the cut but still highly considered were men like George W. Truett, R. G. Lee, W. A. Criswell, and Gardner Taylor.

The final list, voted on by *Preaching Magazine's* board of contributing editors, included the following preachers ranked from the most influential on the church and on the wider society: 1. James S. Stewart (1896–1990); 2. Billy Graham (1918–); 3. George Butterick (1892–1980); 4. Martin Luther King Jr. (1929–1968); 5. Harry Emerson Fosdick (1878–1969); 6. G. Campbell Morgan (1863–1945); 7. William E. Sangster (1900–1960); 8. John R. W. Stott (1921–); 9. D. Martyn Lloyd-Jones (1899–1981); and 10. Clarence Macartney (1879–1957).

Let's consider several of these. James Stewart is considered the best of these preachers. Stewart was a New Testament scholar who taught at the University of Edinburgh. He was primarily an expository preacher. He was known as an articulate, persuasive, conscience-piercing, God-exalting preacher. His driving passion was world evangelism.[71]

Billy Graham has preached to more people in person than anyone in history. His preaching is direct and simple, filled with illustrations and application. As a rule, he begins his sermons by inviting his hearers to come to Christ. His singular purpose is to compel people to come to Christ.

Martin Luther King Jr., preacher and civil rights leader, was articulate and passionate as he spoke. He had almost a lyrical quality in his delivery. His illustrations and application were masterful. He represents the best qualities of the African American preacher.

John R. W. Stott and Martyn Lloyd-Jones, both preachers in London, held long and distinguished pastorates. Both, though, may be remembered for their writings on preaching. Both published works that are considered

---

71 Michael Duduit, "The Ten Greatest Preachers of the Twentieth Century" at Preaching.com

classics. Lloyd-Jones penned *Preaching and Preachers*. Stott authored *Between Two Worlds*.

Three more preachers deserve mention. Two teachers of preaching who have also been masterful in their preaching are Warren Wiersbe and Haddon Robinson. Every preacher should read Wiersbe's *Listening to the Giants* and *Walking with the Giants*. For a generation, Robinson's *Biblical Preaching* has been a standard textbook in the field of homiletics.

It is the opinion of this author that the most effective preacher in the latter part of the twentieth century and the beginning of the twenty-first century is Charles Stanley (1932–). Through his "In Touch" television and radio ministry as well as his pulpit at the First Baptist Church in Atlanta, more people have heard the gospel from his lips than any other preacher in history.

The purist expository preachers at the conclusion of the twentieth and beginning of the twenty-first century in my estimate are Jerry Vines (1937–), past pastor of the First Baptist Church of Jacksonville, Florida, and David Jeremiah of Shadow Mountain Church in San Diego, California. Their sermons deserve to be studied and emulated. Vines' *Power in the Pulpit* written with Jim Shaddix is well worth studying.

Finally, I would be remiss if I neglected to mention Jerry Falwell as one of history's great preachers. Not always expository, but always biblical and thematic, many consider him the greatest leader in evangelical Christianity at the conclusion of the twentieth and beginning of the twenty-first centuries.

Space does not permit me to include any more preachers in this overview of the history of preaching. As we turn our attention to the priority and particulars of connecting with our listeners, consider five common traits of all great preachers.

First, they were confident of their salvation and of their call to preach. Second, they believed that God spoke through His Word and as such had great confidence in Scripture. Third, they were all disciplined and invested great time and energy in the preparation and delivery of themselves and their sermons. Fourth, they had great confidence that God spoke through them. Fifth, they had a great conviction that they must preach for a verdict. The response of their hearers had eternal significance. Each of these qualities can be developed and enhanced. I challenge you to study the great preachers of history and let them mentor you to become a more effective communicator of the gospel.

Chapter 7

Connecting with Those Who Listen

Great preachers in history have all had the common denominator of being able to connect with their listeners. Concerning Jesus, history tells us that "the common people heard Him gladly." It was true of Chrysostom, Augustine, Luther, Zwingli, and myriads of other notable preachers in history. In fact, it is true of all great communicators.[72]

So the critical question is, "How do I connect with my listeners?" Or better, "How can I learn to connect?" All across the world, sermons are preached weekly that leave listeners unmoved, unimpressed, uninspired, unmotivated, and unchanged. In the words of Scripture, "Brethren, these things ought not be."[73]

According to John Maxwell, "Connecting is the ability to identify with people and relate to them in a way that increases your influence with them." From the preacher's perspective, it is living and speaking in such a way that people are transformed through the renewing of their minds, hearts, and wills. Connecting deals with a variety of issues: credibility, commitment, cognition, content, and creativity. It also deals with delivery, but we shall address that in a later chapter. Since we cannot influence people without connecting with them, let's consider the issues related to connecting. How can we be more effective in connecting with our listeners? [74]

---

72 Mark 12:37.
73 James 3:10.
74 John C. Maxwell, *Everyone Communicates, Few Connect* (Nashville: Thomas Nelson, 2010), 3.

Credibility Issues

When it comes to speaking in public, and preaching in particular, people are not asking, "Is the message true or real?" but "Are you true or real?" I am writing about your credibility. Do you authentically live what you say you believe? The essence of hypocrisy is the attempt to promote something you do not embrace yourself. I am writing about your credibility. Credibility is that curious mixture of character, competence, and consistency.

The first concern, here, is character. Do you live what you preach? Are you growing in your walk with God? Nathaniel Hawthorne put it this way: "No man can for any considerable time wear one face to himself and another to the multitude without finally getting bewildered as to which is the true one." Speaking of the importance of character, basketball legend John Wooden observed, "Ability will get you to the top, but it takes character to keep you there." Phillips Brooks, the great Episcopal preacher, made this declaration:[75]

> Do not pray for easy lives; pray to be stronger people! Do
> not pray for tasks equal to your powers; pray for powers
> equal to your tasks. Then the doing of your work shall be
> no miracle, but you shall be a miracle. Every day you shall
> wonder at yourself, at the richness of life which has come
> to you by the grace of God. [76]

I am not saying that you are completely mature. I am saying that you are on the journey to maturity and that your character is becoming more and more like Christ. As you preach, share your journey; share your struggles and weaknesses. Share where you are making progress. Share what you are learning. Your listeners do not expect you to be perfect. They do expect you to be authentic.

I remember Rick Warren saying once, "The messenger authenticates the message." And perhaps we need to be reminded of John Maxwell's words: "If you want to impact people, don't talk about your successes; talk about your failures." He also observed, "Connecting isn't primarily about learning to become a better presenter. It's about becoming the kind of person others want to connect with." Citing Parker Palmer, Maxwell concludes, "The people with whom we have deepest connection are those who acknowledge their weaknesses."[77]

---

75   Edward K. Rowell, ed., *Quotes and Idea Starters* (Grand Rapids: Baker Book House, 1996), 19.
76   Ibid., 20
77   Maxwell, 139, 194, 240

Credibility starts with character, but it also requires a measure of competence. Can you speak from a position of authority? Do you know what you are talking about? Do you have a track record of accomplishment? Do you have anything to show for your labor? Maxwell put it this way:

> Nothing speaks like results. If you want to build the kind of credibility that connects with people, then deliver results before you deliver a message. Get out there and do what you advise others to do. Communicate from experience.[78]

Character and competency are important, but the third requirement for credibility is consistency. Have you demonstrated character and competency over the long haul? It is the little things done well over a long period of time that demonstrates consistency. As a pastor, teacher, and coach, I remind my listeners that champions are made in the off season. When others slack off, the champion is hard at work preparing for the challenges ahead.

One of my heroes is Jonathan Edwards. He was a living demonstration of credibility. He was a man of sterling character who was incredibly competent. And he demonstrated over the long haul, through seasons of great blessing as well as seasons of great adversity, the authenticity of his walk with God. Like Edwards, if we are going to connect with our listeners, it starts with the foundation of credibility.[79] If we are going to connect with our listeners, we must demonstrate a two-fold commitment: first, to our Lord, then to our listeners.

Out of our commitment to Jesus Christ arises both our purpose and passion. If our purpose is like Paul's, "to be pleasing to Him," then our purpose will translate into a passion to do those things that please our Lord. As a preacher of the gospel, do you have a passion for the Lord and His work? Maxwell asks a series of questions about this: Do I believe what I say? Has the message I preached changed me? "Do I believe this message will help others? Have I seen it change others?" True commitment to the Lord translates into purpose and passion for the Lord and His work.[80]

Our commitment must also be toward the people who are our listeners. I tell my students over and over, "People do not care how much you know

---

78 Ibid., p. 243

79 See John Piper, *The Supremacy of God in Preaching* (Grand Rapids: Baker Book House), 1990.

80 2 Corinthians 5:9b; Maxwell, 213.

until they know how much you care." Commitment to our hearers will translate into two disciplines. First, I will work to build a rapport with my listeners, and second, I will work in my preparation before I speak to them publicly.

Consider the need for building a rapport with your listeners. Even before you step into the pulpit, it is wise to work at building relationships with your listeners. My first interim pastorate was at the North Main Baptist Church in Danville, Virginia. I did five things to try to build rapport with the people in our congregation. First, I walked around the auditorium before each service greeting people, shaking hands, giving hugs. Second, I went to every adult Bible study class every Sunday morning and just told the folks I was glad they were there. Third, I spent time with staff. We shared a meal at least once a week. Fourth, we ate with church members when invited. And fifth, I consistently took or returned phone calls. Why?

I did all this so I could connect with them and build relationships. In short, you have to win people's hearts before you win their minds. If people believe you care about them, they will be much more apt to listen to what you have to say. And if what you have to say is important, then it is worth working at building relationships. Maxwell asserts that people are asking three questions about the speaker: Do you care for me? Can you help me? And can I trust you? Hopefully, the answer to all three will be yes.[81]

Commitment toward your listeners is not only demonstrated in how well you build rapport, but it is also demonstrated in how well you prepare before you speak. People can quickly tell if you are winging it and if you are unprepared. It takes time and energy to prepare to speak to a group or preach to a congregation. Part of your commitment is demonstrated in your willingness to work at preparation. And when it comes to preparation, there are cognitive issues that must be addressed.

Cognitive Issues

By cognitive issues, I am writing about how you see, how you think, how you discern, how you process the environment, and the information you wish to communicate.

Before you ever preach a word, you need to be concerned about the environment: the sound, the lights, and the proximity of the preacher to the congregation. You need to look for any obstacles that might hinder

---

81   Maxwell, 38, 40–41.

your best opportunity to connect with your listeners. Are any barriers present that you will have to overcome? Sometimes a huge pulpit can create a psychological barrier between you and the listeners. So, your first task is to minimize anything that would hinder your ability to connect.

Next, you need to work at understanding how the people you are speaking to listen and learn. Some are auditory learners. They want information. They want you to explain the text. Others are visual learners. They need analogies, anecdotes, and illustrations. Others are kinesthetic learners. They need to participate. They want application; the more the better. Others are tactile learners, but that plays a very minor role in the preaching event. It can help you be more effective if you have some idea of how your people listen and learn. [82]

Every listener has what educators call an RAS—a Reticular Activation System. This is that part of the brain that screens out what it perceives as useless information. So what gets our attention? Things we value or find interesting, things we believe are unusual, and things that threaten us get our attention. As you plan your preaching, you must work at crafting messages that can bypass the Reticular Activation System. [83]

The way I do this is that I visualize the people I am preaching to and I ask the questions: What do they care about? What are they concerned with? What causes them to worry? What are their fears? What are their priorities? I view the answers to these questions as the things inside their concern zone. Anything outside their concern zone, they are apathetic about. To connect with people, you must start where they are.

This process, for me, is a playing out of my core questions. Before I ever speak anywhere, I ask these three questions. To whom am I speaking? What are their needs? And what does God say? Every wise preacher must learn to ask the right questions.

My first question is always, "To whom am I speaking?" This will be a key to knowing what to say and how to say it. I want to know their spiritual condition, their maturity level, and their values.

Several years ago, I was invited to preach at a church in east Tennessee. The pastor wanted to use the night as an evangelistic emphasis where members would invite lost friends and hopefully we would see a harvest of new believers. Just to be safe, I prepared two messages. The first was

---

82 Al Fasol, Roy Fish, Steve Gaines and Ralph Douglas West, *Preaching Evangelistically* (Nashville: B&H, 2006), 107–08.

83 Herschel W. York and Bert Decker, *Preaching with Bold Assurance* (Nashville: B&H, 2003), 207–09.

evangelistic in nature. The second was on the need for the church to fully engage in fulfilling the Great Commission.

When I arrived, the church was pretty packed, and a sense of excitement and anticipation was in the air. After the music portion of the service, it was my turn. Before I preached, I asked the people present to bow their heads. Then, I asked this question: "If you are here tonight and you know there has been a time in your life when you have invited Christ to come into your life to be your Lord and Savior, would you slip up your hand?" I was not surprised that every person I saw in the room slipped up their hand. After a word of prayer, I preached the sermon on the Great Commission. Why preach an evangelistic message if everyone already claims to be saved? It helps to know who you are speaking to.

My second question when preparing to preach is, "What are their needs?" This is key to connecting to people. We must address them at their point of need.

When Jesus began His public ministry, He went to the synagogue in Nazareth and read the passage out of Isaiah, "The Spirit of the Lord is upon Me, Because He has anointed me to preach the gospel to the poor. He has sent Me to proclaim release to the captives, and recovery of sight to the blind, to set free those who are downtrodden, to proclaim the favorable year of the Lord." He then said, "Today this Scripture has been fulfilled in your hearing." Notice that Jesus addresses five points of need as He declares His purpose. [84]

A wise preacher will look for the needs among his listeners and address the gospel message to those needs. Maxwell advises speakers to link what they say with what people need. He points out that we connect with people by focusing on them and their needs. My friend Freddie Gage has told me often that if we preach to human needs, we will never lack an audience. So look for people's needs, hurts, concerns, and issues.

I have heard people criticize "needs-based" preaching as superficial and shallow. My response to them is that if you will study the sermons of Moses, Jesus, and Paul, you will discover that human need was often the point of contact for applying the truth of God's Word. According to Rick Warren, everybody needs to have their faith reinforced, their hope renewed, and their love restored. [85] Of course, this leads into my third key question.

My next key question is, "What does God say?" My preaching is, as I tell my students, "Anchored in the text, surfaces from the text, and is

---

84 Luke 4:17–21.
85 Rick Warren, Saddleback Seminars, "How to Communicate to Change Lives." n.d.

driven by the text." The Word of God is the Spirit's instrument for effective change. So every sermon, every message must communicate, "This is what God says!" And the Spirit of God will give you and lead you to the right text for the right moment.

The reason I ask these three questions is because I want to communicate effectively with my listeners. I want to connect. These are the ways I think through and pray through my sermon preparation before I ever say a word. In my preparation, I am also thinking of the content of my message.

Content Issues

When it comes to preparing the content of the message, the preacher must constantly be thinking of connecting with his listeners.

In the introduction, the preacher should, among other things, communicate the benefit, the payoff, the take home. "This is how today's message will help you." I will say much more about the introduction later. Good evangelists, like Junior Hill or Billy Graham, will introduce their invitation at the beginning of their message. If we do not connect in the first three minutes, chances are the listener will check out and not be listening. Maxwell quotes Myrna Murphy, who says, "People have remote controls in their heads today. If you don't catch their interest, they just click you off." So, we must plan and work to gain and maintain attention from the outset.[86]

As we develop the content of our messages, we must connect on three levels: intellectually, emotionally, and volitionally. We connect intellectually as we communicate what the text says and means. We are communicating on an understanding level. This requires clarity of thought and expression on our part. Sometimes it requires repetition so that people "get it." Remember that in the end, people are not persuaded by our words but by what they have understood. I teach my students that illustrations are like windows and mirrors. Windows let light in, and mirrors help us see ourselves. All of this is for the purpose of understanding. In every message I prepare, I ask, what are the essential truths that I must communicate to bring about understanding?[87]

We must also connect on an emotional level. We want people to feel truth the way we feel it. Counselors talk about how there are eight basic emotions: gladness, sadness, loneliness, fear, anger, hurt, shame, and guilt.

---

86 Maxwell, 179.
87 Ibid., 165.

Each of these can be brought in to play as you develop your message. Emotions help people connect with you. You want them to feel what you feel.

Recently I preached a series of messages on the life of David from 1 and 2 Samuel. One message was on 2 Samuel 11 and 12 where David committed adultery with Bathsheba. I entitled it "Consequences and Mercy." If you recall, part of the consequence of David's sin was that Bathsheba conceived and had a son. We are free to choose our actions, but we are not free to choose the consequences. Part of David's punishment was that God took the child. David repented, fasted, prayed, and begged God to spare the child's life. Yet, God took him. At the child's death, David declared, "I will go to him, but he will never return to me."[88]

In order for our people to grasp the gravity of that statement and the hope it holds, I shared a story from my time as pastor in Nashville. For months, Marci and Seton Tomyn were looking forward to the arrival of their next child, Joshua. It was a problem pregnancy, and Marci was confined to bed rest the last trimester before delivery. On his birthday, everything went according to plan, no complications. Everyone was relieved.

On their second day home, Joshua quit nursing and began to run a fever. The pediatrician sent them to Vanderbilt's neonatal intensive care unit where he was diagnosed with a severe staph infection. Five weeks after his admission to the hospital, we were having staff meeting. A knock came on the door, and Seton was told that he had an important phone call from the doctor. When Seton returned to the room about ten minutes later, his face was ashen white. He sat down, put his head in his hands, and began to sob. When he finally regained his composure, he said, "The doctor just told me that my son is brain-dead." It was an awful moment. The grief in the room was thick enough to cut it with a knife.

A few days later, I had the sad honor of preaching Joshua's funeral service. My text was 2 Samuel 12:23b and the hope we have of seeing him again. David's grief has ministered to multitudes who have lost little children. And everyone in the room felt the pain and the grief and the hope and confident expectation that we would see little Joshua again. No doubt, we connected on an emotional level.

Yet, we also need to connect on a volitional level. This goes beyond application, although it includes application. It says here is what you do with what I have said. In Maxwell's words, it goes from "know how" to "do now." It involves persuasion. It also involves encouragement. Many

---

88 2 Samuel 12:23b.

times in messages, I have noted, "This is what you can do." Then I tell the folks, "You can do this!" I explain that God will never make a demand that He will not give grace to accomplish. I let them know I believe in them and that they indeed can do what I have shared. Steve Jobs once said, "Leadership is about inspiring people to do the things they never thought they could."[89]

Planning your content so that you connect with your listeners requires that you get their attention at the outset, communicate the benefits, and address your listeners on an intellectual, emotional, and volitional level. It means settling for nothing less than changed lives. Preaching to connect has one more element that I consider vital. It requires creativity on the preacher's part.

Creativity Issues

At this point, I am back to asking questions. When I want to connect, I need to be considering an additional set of issues that will help me refine my message. I remember hearing someone say that we are not preaching the Bible to people but we are preaching to people about themselves from the Bible. If that is the case, then I must work to connect the listener and the truth of the text. That being the case, here are seven questions that will spur our creativity in communication.

What is the most creative way to say this? The less I am predictable in what I say, the greater the potential for impact. One year I did a Christmas series of messages on "The Emotion of Christmas." I looked through the eyes of Mary, Joseph, the shepherds, the wise men, Simeon, and Anna. In the sermon on Mary, I talked about loneliness. I talked about false accusations and ostracism. I talked about being an outcast for the sake of Jesus. The creative revisiting of Mary's experience connected. Of course, my point was the people of Bible days are no different than we are when it comes to emotions.[90]

I remember preaching a series on the family we called "Life in America with Dick and Jane." We traced Dick and Jane from their childhood until Jane's death in a series of dramatic sketches that set up the sermons. It was amazing to see Dick and Jane age over the weeks. Another time, as I mentioned earlier, I preached a series of messages on "How to Survive a Very Bad Day." It was a revisiting of Jesus' seven last words on the cross.

---

89   Maxwell, 223, 205–06.
90   These seven questions are not original. I heard them in Rick Warren's Saddleback Seminar on "How to Communicate to Change Lives."

We packaged it in a survival series mode where Brent Gambrell played a knock-off of Steve Erwin searching for wild game. All of this and many more series were the creative effort of a great team.

What is the most encouraging way to say this? My goal was not so much to say how things are but to communicate how they could be. Proverbs 12:25 says, "Anxiety in a man's heart weighs it down, but a good word (encouragement) cheers it up." Our goal in preaching is to lift people up, communicate what God has done for them, and explain to them what they can be. We want to focus on potential. No wonder 1 Thessalonians 4:18 says, "Encourage one another." We are encouraged when we are reminded of what God has done and what He still wants to do.

What is the most interesting way to say this? Good delivery helps make sermons interesting. Illustrations can also rouse the interest level. Learn to tell stories. Use humor. All of these are ways that bring additional interest.

John Maxwell discusses his criterion for a quote or illustration. He says it must fit one or more of four categories: Humor—something that will make people laugh; Heart—something that will captivate people's attention; Hope—something that will inspire people; and Help—something that will assist people in a tangible way. Each of these are for the purpose of maintaining interest.[91]

What is the most personal way to say it? The highest impact comes when people share their hearts. A generation ago, homiletics professors warned against using personal illustrations. The mantra was, "It is not about you." Over the last thirty years, however, communicators have learned the value of personal illustrations. If we connect with people, they will identify with us. And that identifying helps them embrace what we say. It cuts through that Reticular Activation System. Share your heart!

Let me give a brief warning about self-disclosure. It can be overdone. If your failures, sins, faults, and shortcomings are so severe that they undermine your credibility, take it to a counselor, take it to the Lord, but do not take it into the pulpit. That is a recipe for disaster.

What is the most positive way to say it? On a positive-negative scale, preaching that is positive is more effective at facilitating change. In Rick Warren's words, "You don't lift people up by putting them down." When we go on the attack mode (not about issues but about people), barriers go up.

One of the hot-button issues of our day is how to address the sin and bondage of homosexuality. I have heard some preachers address this issue

---

91   Maxwell, 152.

with scathing attacks. I do not believe they were very effective at helping their folks find deliverance and salvation. In contrast, those who say, "There is hope, and there is deliverance. Christ understands, and He can make you brand new," get a better hearing. After all, Jesus loves each of us, and He wants us to experience His forgiveness and freedom. In short, we can give them hell or give them help. I do not believe we can do both. By the way, we should preach against sin with a broken heart, with humility, and with hope. In short, we should preach the positive alternative, for what is right and not just against what is wrong. After all, the Gospel is "good news"!

What is the most practical way to say it? This is directly related to application. If our goal is changed lives, then we must give our people steps of action, a game plan, a way out, a how-to. When Jesus gave the Great Commission, His instruction after we make disciples is "teaching them to observe whatever I have commanded you." That means doing what He said. Tell people, "Here is what you can do." Then help them see what needs to be done. I recently preached a series of messages on the church out of Ephesians. At the conclusion of the series, I said, "Now in light of what God says about the church, here are six steps you can take as a church to make this a reality in this place." And I laid it out one step at a time.

In our preaching, we should always aim at some specific step of obedience. It is wise to tell your people why they should do it. Then show them how they can do it. I recently attended a series of conference meetings that promoted all the new tools of technology available for professors. What I noticed about the content was that it was long on "ought to" and short on "how to." If we are going to help people change, we must show them how to do what is expected.

And finally, what is the simplest way to say it? Jesus was simple in what He said. Peter was simple. Paul was simple most of time. I am not saying simple-minded. I am saying communicate in a way that people understand. Albert Einstein once said, "If you can't explain it simply, you don't understand it enough." [92]

Remember, our goal in communicating is to connect with people so we can share the life-transforming truth of who Jesus is and what He can do. We want to connect so that people might be changed. And it all starts when we make the decision and implement a plan to help us connect with our listeners.

---

92   Ibid., 151.

Chapter 8

The Ingredients of a Great Sermon

Just like a great meal requires great ingredients or a custom-built house requires superior building materials, a great sermon requires great ingredients. So, in preaching, what are those ingredients?

My assumption is that great sermons require credible spokesmen. As we have seen earlier, this requires a combination of credibility, character, competence, integrity, transparency, authority, and humility.

In order to become a credible spokesman, four words of advice might prove helpful. First, we must live the life. Although many professions are not necessarily affected by a person's character, the ministry is not one of them. As Warren Wiersbe observes, "The work that the pastor does cannot be separated from the life he lives." He continues, "Unless the truth is written on the pastor's heart and revealed in his life, he can never write it on the hearts of others."[93]

Second, be yourself. All too often ministers try to copy other ministers. God does not need duplicates. He creates originals. Spurgeon writes, "Some men never can do much for God in the way which they prefer, for they were never cut out for the work." In other words, a minister ought to do what God has equipped him to do. Spurgeon continues, "Let each man find out what God wants him to do, and then let him do it or die in the attempt." As a minister, do not try to copy another man's ministry. Rather, ask God what He would have you do as a unique individual. [94]

---

93 Warren Wiersbe, *Listening to the Giants* (Grand Rapids: Baker Book House, 1980), 345.
94 Charles H. Spurgeon, *An All-Round Ministry* (London: Banner of Truth, reprinted 1972), 232–33.

③ Third, trust the Lord. It sounds so easy, but oftentimes ministers trust themselves and worry. Brown, Clinard, and Northcutt wrote about power in preaching. Pointing out that power does not come from sermon preparation, they suggest that it does require a confidence and belief in preaching. It rests upon the content of the sermon and upon the character of the man who preaches. But all this is not enough, they maintain. It absolutely depends upon the work of the Holy Spirit. And the power of the Spirit rests upon the man who is dedicated to and dependent upon the Lord. [95]

④ Finally, it requires hard work. Alton McEachern writes, "No preacher is to be judged simply upon the basis of his gifts or charisma, but on the basis of what he has done with them." He concludes, "Whether the preacher has one or ten talents, he is to dedicate his whole personality to the work of preaching and being a faithful pastor."[96]

Once we have a credible spokesman, then we can begin to examine the ingredients of great sermons. When my students in the course "Great Preachers and Their Preaching" assess sermons from history, this is the checklist we use. I also challenge my students to evaluate their own preaching using this checklist. So what are the ingredients of a great sermon?

A Clear Biblical Message

The first ingredient of a great sermon is that it has a clear biblical message. It is not a talk or devotional thought. It is not a collection of clever ideas or simply moving stories. It is a message that is anchored in the Word, surfaces from the Word, and is driven by the Word.

Normative for every preacher is Paul's admonition to Timothy where he wrote, "Preach the word; be ready in season and out of season; reprove, rebuke, exhort, with great patience and instruction." Here Paul communicates the preacher's first duty is to preach the Word. The world does not need our opinions. It does need to know the heart and mind of God as He has revealed it in His Word. [97]

The preacher is responsible for communicating what the text says, what the text means, and what it demands. Unless a sermon communicates clearly biblical truth, it is not a sermon. Great sermons are built upon a

---

95 H. C. Brown, H. Gordon Clinard, and Jesse Northcutt, *Steps to the Sermon* (Nashville: Broadman Press, 1963), 194–96.

96 Alton McEachern, *Proclaim the Gospel* (Nashville: Convention Press, 1975), 30.

97 2 Timothy 4:2 (NASB).

clear biblical message. If the message is not clear or the message is not biblical, it is not a sermon.

God has promised that His Word will not return void. He has promised to bless the communicator of His Word. The first ingredient of a great sermon is that it has a clear biblical message.

Connecting the Truth of Scripture with People's Lives

A second ingredient of a great sermon is that it connects the truth of Scripture with where people live. It is more than just an explanation of a Bible passage. It intentionally creates a connection with the world of the Bible and the present condition of humanity.

John Stott said that preaching is building a bridge between two worlds, the past and the present; not just vague references to modern times but to the specifics of today's challenges. What does God say to us today? What issues does He want addressed today? It is connecting not just preacher to people but God and His truth to our daily lives.

I believe we have failed miserably if people leave our services and sermons and are not thinking, "This is what God says about my life right now." It is the preacher's task to make that connection.

Vivid Illustrations

A third ingredient is that great sermons use vivid illustrations. As I have said before, illustrations are like windows and mirrors. They let in light, and they show us ourselves.

Illustrations take numerous forms. Quotations containing profound insight and thoughts have been used for centuries. Pictures from everyday life teach us through what Wayne McDill identifies as natural analogies.[98] Recall Jesus' explanation of the work of a preacher, "A sower went out to sow." Jesus often told stories to illustrate what He wanted to communicate. Recall the parables of the lost silver, lost sheep, and lost son of Luke 15. Or recall the parable of the good Samaritan.

Illustrations help bring clarity and understanding, particularly to the application of the sermon's text.

Let me give four cautions in the use of illustrations. First, they need to be accurate. Check and double-check your facts. Usually if an illustration sounds too good to be true, it is. When we use illustrations that are untrue

---

98 Wayne McDill, *12 Essential Skills for Great Preaching* (Nashville: B&H, 2006), 138–50.

or inaccurate, we hurt our own credibility. Next, make sure the illustration is descriptive of a truth you are communicating. Do not tell a story or use an illustration just because it is good. Always make sure it is making a point.

A third caution is that it needs to be appropriate. If the illustration does not really fit, save it for another day. Do not use it just because it is hot. We can waste illustrations if we attempt to force them where they really do not apply.

And fourth, make sure your illustration is timely. Does it fit the occasion? I have a friend who is a nationally known speaker. For years, he worked to get me to use more humor. My challenge came in that some of the humor he wanted me to use was often not timely. I have great appreciation for his willingness to help. But make sure the illustration will help and not leave a negative impression or hurt what you are trying to accomplish. As a preacher, that is your call.

An ingredient of all great sermons is that they use effectively and appropriately vivid illustrations.

Practically Applied

The fourth ingredient of a great sermon is that it is practically applied. It is incredibly important that our people know not just what the text says and means but also how it applies to their lives. Some sermons that are expositional masterpieces with wonderful illustrations fail at this juncture because the preacher fails to drive home the application.

Every sermon should answer a minimum of two questions. First, what does God expect me to do in light of this text? And second, how do I do it? Whatever the subject might be, these two issues should always be addressed.

I teach my students that their sermons should always fall into one of three broad categories. First, it might be an evangelistic message. We see examples of this both in Peter's preaching at Pentecost and Paul's preaching in Athens. Second, we have edification messages to believers teaching them how to live out the Christian life. Most of the New Testament is a demonstration of this. And third, I am convinced that preachers have an obligation to address the great moral issues of the day. In short, they are addressing the culture and communicating God's standards and demands. Each of these categories carries an almost automatic set of applications. We want lost people to be saved. "Here is what you must do." We want believers to grow spiritually. "Here is what you must do." We want our nation to embrace biblical standards of morality. "Here is how this can be done." Application says, "This is what you must do!"

Organized with a Logical Flow

A fifth ingredient in a great sermon is that it is organized with a logical flow. It makes sense. It follows a logical development.

Several years ago, my wife and I visited New York City, where our youngest daughter was working. On Sunday, our daughter took us to a very prominent church with a famous pastor. The sermon that day was from a single text in the Old Testament approximately six verses long. As the sermon progressed, the preacher jumped back and forth, pointing out something from the top, the bottom, the middle. He so jumped around his text that no one could follow him. He would have communicated much more effectively if he had started at the beginning of his text and worked his way through it in a systematic way following the logical flow of the text at hand.

Remember, people are not changed by the words we say but by what they understand of the words we say. If the sermon has a logical development of key ideas all reinforcing the principal theme or big idea, the listeners are much more apt to "get it." It takes work on the part of the preacher to organize his message in a logical way.

In assessing a sermon, we should ask, "Does each point connect to the whole?" "Can the listener see and understand how each part connects?" "Does this sermon and its outline lead to a logical climax?" If sermons are not organized with a logical flow, they are substandard.

Balanced

A sixth ingredient of a great sermon is that it is balanced. Appropriate attention is given to explanation, illustration, argumentation (when necessary), and application. The major points are symmetrical and reinforce the principal theme of the text.

I have heard sermons and sadly have preached some where the first two, three, or four points are in balance. Each point may have taken five to eight minutes to develop. All of a sudden, I looked up and realized I'm out of time so I summarize the last point or two in a minute. The result is a sermon out of balance. Not good!

I have heard other sermons that spend an inordinate amount of time with explanation with almost no illustrations or application. Nice lecture but not a life-changing Word from God!

I do have some friends who champion the one-point sermon. These are problematic to me because as a rule, the listeners are not grasping the flow of Scripture as it unfolds in the text. Although the preacher is preaching for "life-change" and focusing on a single idea, too often, it is not connected with the bigger picture of Scripture and its context. For me, these sermons lack balance.

Relevant

A seventh ingredient of a great sermon is that it is relevant to the lives of the listener. By relevant, I mean that it addresses specific issues that people are dealing with now. It gives help and hope. This is especially true during times of crisis.

The Sunday after September 11, 2001, our church was packed. Our Senator, Fred Thompson, made some comments about the tragedy, and I was appreciative that he thought enough of us to address our people and the people of our state. But our folks wanted to know, "Does God have anything to say to us about this tragedy?" Needless to say, I dropped what I had planned to say and preached a message on what God wants us to know. I addressed specific steps of what people could do.

Here is a rule of thumb. If your people are preoccupied with an issue, you probably ought to preach on it. Relevant preaching targets what is in people's concern zone. If the presence of need is a key to what God wants to say, then do not miss the opportunity. What good will it do if you preach a great message that no one cares about? Now I realize that needs come on multiple levels: felt, real, and spiritual. It is imperative that we do not take the most relevant message in the world and make it irrelevant by neglect.

The ability to preach relevant messages depends on our willingness to understand our people and their needs and our world and its needs. That is one reason that it is vitally important for the preacher to be a student of God's Word, people, and the world around him. That is why it is important for the preacher to be ready and study and meditate and pray. These are disciplines that assist the preacher to keep his messages relevant.

Well Delivered

An eighth ingredient of a great sermon is that it is well delivered. Sermons are intended to be communicated verbally. This is a discipline in oral communication. It is tragic when a well-crafted, prayed-over, well-balanced, inspirational sermon is made boring because a preacher fails to deliver the message effectively. Delivery is a discipline that every preacher can work on. Removing distracting mannerisms may be a challenge, but it is a challenge worth embracing. It has a payoff for hard work.

Several key components comprise the most important facets of delivery. The first is the fact that the preacher needs to make eye contact. Two issues arise here. First, the preacher must be familiar enough with his material that he is not tied to his notes. When my students preach in class, I allow them to take one page of notes. The reason? So they do not stand there reading their sermons to those who listen.

Second, making eye contact helps the preacher connect with his listeners. I would think something was wrong if I were talking with someone and he or she refused to look at me. If a preacher does not look at the congregation, I think something is wrong as well. My suggestion is that the preacher make eye contact with someone in the congregation and maintain it anywhere from ten to thirty seconds. Let them know you are talking to them personally. In a large room, the preacher can systematically work his way across the congregation one side to the other. In very large rooms with cameras and large screens, people who sit more than five rows back as a rule are watching the screen. If the preacher wants to make eye contact with most of the room, he will look right into the camera while he preaches. Charles Stanley is a master at this.

Besides eye contact, the preacher needs to maintain what my professors used to call full vocal production. Speak out of your diaphragm and project. With your voice, you can vary your rate, pitch, and volume. Work at being articulate.

Another component of delivery is the need to use appropriate gestures. Use gestures to emphasize what you are saying. Remember that the larger the room you are preaching in, the larger or grander your gestures need to be. I tell my students if they want to learn how not to do gestures then watch car salesmen on television. They seem to be the world's worst. Let your gestures reinforce what you are saying.

Great preachers preaching great sermons know how to use what we call dramatic pauses. When you make a key point or say something significant, pause for a moment and let it sink in.

The last thing I want to say about delivery is that the preacher must work to minimize distracting mannerisms. I suggest you record yourself on camera, then critique your delivery. Do you have any distracting mannerisms? I have seen students shuffle their feet, play with the change in their pockets, scratch their temple, and the list can go on and on. Surprisingly, most people are unaware of their distracting mannerisms until they see it for themselves. Remember, great sermons are well delivered.

Preaching for a Verdict

The ninth ingredient of a great sermon is that the preacher is preaching for a verdict. His intention is to persuade his listeners not only on the truth of what he is saying but also of the importance of responding, surrendering, starting, or stopping now.

Great preachers create a sense of vital urgency when they speak. This is more than saying this is what you need to do. It is insisting that you do it now. It is marshalling their arguments in such a way that the listener feels compelled to respond.

I recall being at the Southern Baptist Convention Pastor's Conference the year that W. A. Criswell preached his historic sermon, "Whether We Live or Whether We Die." By the end of the sermon, the pastors were persuaded that we must see the conservative resurgence through to its conclusion. We were convinced that to fail to do this would mean death to the convention. He preached for a verdict. Every great sermon is preached for a verdict.

Anointed by the Spirit

The tenth ingredient of a great sermon is that it is anointed by the Holy Spirit. This means simply that when the sermon is preached, the Holy Spirit bears witness to it with conviction in the hearts and minds of the listeners. Recall how Jesus told us that when He (Jesus) departs, He will send the Spirit who will bear witness of Jesus, be the Helper, convict the world of sin, righteousness, and judgment, guide His followers with His truth, disclose what is ours because of Jesus, and glorify Jesus.[99]

So the question is, how do we appropriate what the Lord has provided? I suggest three steps. First, pray over your sermons as you prepare them. Ask the Lord to guide your study from start to finish. Ask for discernment as you prepare and power as you deliver the message. Ask your listeners to pray for you. Ask the Lord to anoint your work.

Step two is that we need to purpose in our hearts to live pure. I love the promise of 1 John 1:9, "If we confess our sins, He is faithful and just

---

99   John 15:27; 16:7–8, 13–14.

to forgive us our sin and cleanse us from all unrighteousness." The secret to purity is staying close to the Lord. We must be careful to neither quench nor grieve the Holy Spirit. [100]

I believe a third step is that we pay the price to prepare to preach. It was said of Spurgeon that he was more concerned to prepare himself than to prepare his message. Of course, I believe that both are important—a prepared messenger and a prepared message.

These are ten ingredients of a great sermon. I challenge you to use these ten as a checklist as you prepare to preach. Also, evaluate sermons you hear, watch, or read by these ten ingredients. I will say more about many of these ingredients in the pages to follow.

In the next chapter, we are going to examine a process for putting these ingredients together to make a strong biblical sermon. Great ingredients are not a substitute for the hard work of preparation. Neither do they guarantee that the sermon will be great.

---

100 Ephesians 4:30, 1 Thessalonians 5:19.

Chapter 9

The Process of Sermon Preparation

If the ingredients for a great sermon are assembled, the question remains, "How do we put everything together?" How do I prepare this spiritual meal? How do I build this spiritual home? Here, I want to focus on the word *process*. Process, like time, is the unfolding sequence of events. So how can you ensure that you are doing the best job of facilitating the process?

When I was learning to preach, the closest I came to learning a process was in reading Criswell's *Guidebook for Pastors* when he advocated, "Save your mornings for God." This was good advice as far as it went. But the question remains. In light of the fact that Sunday is on the way (it is always on the way), how do I prepare the message or messages in the time allotted? And I am not even taking into consideration a Wednesday evening sermon or some weekday speaking event.

I have many friends who are senior pastors of great churches. Many of them have reputations for being great preachers. What is surprising is that no two of them have a preparation methodology just like someone else. Each one has adopted a process that works for him. I am going to teach you a process and a method that I have used effectively. I recommend you start with this and then alter it as you see fit. Establish a method that works for you, your schedule, and your routine. Any method is better than no method. Some methods are better than others. Here is one that worked for me. Before we launch into learning a methodology, consider first some preliminary principles.

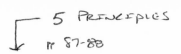

Preliminary Principles

How can you ensure that you are doing the best you can do to facilitate the process?

First, I want to encourage you to make preaching your top priority. I tell my new students at orientation that if they learn everything in every class yet fail to learn to communicate, they will be a failure in ministry. Yet, even with a sound set of skills in the preacher's toolbox, it takes an incredible amount of diligence to perform consistently well in the pulpit.

If a person makes preaching his top priority, several commitments are necessary. First, the preacher must set aside time. Strong biblical sermons take time. The preacher must block off uninterrupted study time. If you examine the great preachers of history, one common denominator is that they all invested time to prepare their messages as well as themselves. Besides time, effective preparation also requires energy. Planning, studying, and preparing take energy. It is hard work. Again, I emphasize that the preacher must give focused, uninterrupted time to his preparation.

My suggestion is that the preacher establish a routine for weekly preparation. That means a consistent time, a consistent place, and a consistent set of steps he follows. I have always preferred to study at home. Whenever we have bought or built a home, we have made sure to have room for a study and for books. I know that many volumes and resources are available online today, but I have always found it more practical for me to have a library from which to work.

Besides making preaching a priority, I want to reiterate that it is important to plan your preaching. The workload of speaking one to six times a week is simply too heavy to wing it. Even preaching once a week effectively is a challenge if it is done well. As I have already said, use a calendar. Keep note of needs, opportunities, and upcoming events. Plan to intersect God's Word and those needs you observe as a pastor.

The next principle I encourage you to embrace is to become preoccupied with Scripture. This looks back to that third question I always ask before speaking to any group, "What does God say?"

As David introduces the Psalms, he writes about the blessed man: "But his delight is in the law of the Lord and in his law he meditates day and night." The more you get the Word in you on a consistent basis, the more effective you will be in the long haul. I suggest to my students that for the first five years of their ministry, they spend a minimum of an hour a day and preferably two simply reading the Scripture. This is for the singular purpose of getting the Word into them. The more we read it, study it, memorize it, meditate on it, and hear it preached, the deeper it will go into our hearts and minds. And the more the Holy Spirit will have to work with.

A fourth principle I encourage you to embrace is to make prayer your constant activity. Paul encouraged the Thessalonians to "pray without ceasing." This is a discipline that any Christian can cultivate. Especially as you prepare your messages, ask the Lord to open your eyes to see the truth, to give you discernment to know how to present it, how to apply it to the needs of your people, and to speak through you as you preach.

The final principle I encourage you to embrace is to depend consistently and consciously upon the Holy Spirit's leading. Live with a sense of calling and expectancy. Whenever we preach, we should expect the Spirit of God to be at work drawing people to Jesus, guiding them to the truth, and bringing conviction. We should be grateful but not surprised when people respond to the preaching of the Word of God.

An Apt Analogy

Preparing a great sermon is like preparing a great meal or building a custom home. It takes great ingredients put together skillfully. Whether cooking, building, or crafting a sermon, the process must follow a sequential pattern. I teach my students that the process of sermon preparation is like building a house.

When I was in college, I built homes. Actually, I was a framing carpenter who worked for a contractor. I became very familiar with the building process. Every house starts with a plan. No one ever goes to a vacant lot, unloads building materials, and then wonders what he or she wants to do. In fact, that is an absurd notion. Every builder starts with plans and permits. Next, the lot is cleared, and the materials, resources, and tools are assembled.

When everything is gathered, the first step is to lay the foundation. It may have a basement. It may be pier and beam. It may be a slab. Different places have different norms. But one principle holds fast. The foundation comes first. In fact, the higher you plan to build, the deeper and stronger the foundation must be.

The next step is to frame up the house according to the plans. Make sure the walls are upright, straight, and braced. Then the decking goes on, and the home is dried in. Note that when the walls go in, each room has a special function: living room, bedrooms, bathrooms, the kitchen, the laundry room, the study. Each room has a function, and it is built according to the plans.

After the house is dried in, the builder proceeds to run the electrical wiring, attach necessary plumbing components, put in various plumbing fixtures, and hang doors and windows. Then comes sheetrock and light fixtures, mudding and painting, hand rails, and the like. The big details are taken care of before the smaller ones.

Cosmetic work, brick, trim, and such come before the final coat of paint. Tile, hardwood, and carpet go in next. Then, you take care of externals like the driveway, landscaping, and seeding the yard.

When everything is cleaned up and prepared, then you turn keys over to the new owners with an invitation to come on in.

This is a very simple description of a process. What I want you to understand is that preparing a biblical sermon well follows a similar process. There are no shortcuts other than as you study Scripture for years you will become more familiar with it and the exegesis time may shorten in length.

The Process of Preparation

I teach my students a ten-step process of sermon preparation. This is one I have followed for years, and it has worked very well for me. I hope it will work for you.

Step one is to select your text with its central idea. If you plan your preaching ahead as I recommend, you should almost never find yourself in a panic mode trying to decide what to preach on next.

If you do short series in the morning, you will hopefully plan so in advance that you know the series, the texts, the titles, and the key ideas months in advance. I believe that the same Holy Spirit who can lead you at the spur of the moment when necessary can lead you months in advance when you get alone with Him and ask for His guidance.

What is good about planning ahead is that you can gather your study materials in advance and not reinvent the wheel, as the old saying goes. It is not unusual for me to have next week's sermon materials sitting out on my desk on Saturday ready to start first thing next Monday.

For those who preach verse by verse, chapter by chapter, and book by book, this same planning works effectively. As I wrote earlier, by the New Year, I would have file folders made up for every sermon I planned to preach in the new year.

Let me remind you that it is easier to deviate from a plan in progress than to always be starting from scratch in your sermon preparation. If you recall, the Sunday after September 11, 2001, I changed my message completely. It was easier to be flexible and on occasion deviate from my plan than to start from square one each week.

Step one in the process is to select the text with its central idea. For most texts, the principal theme or central idea is simple or at least relatively clear. You isolate the subjects, verbs, and objects in the verses. It is usually pretty clear.

② Step two is to do an exegesis of the text. I believe that before you ever attempt to prepare a sermon, you ought to first prepare an exegesis. An exegesis by definition is "the use of critical and scholarly procedures to derive the meaning of a passage of Scripture."[101] A sound exegesis will include minimally a review of the grammar used, explaining any words that might need clarification. It will review the context, genre, syntax, and all issues necessary for clearly exploring what the text says and means. I will go into more detail about exegesis in a later chapter. For preaching through books, I have found Harold Bryson's *Expository Preaching* very helpful.

Before I attempt to prepare any sermon, I always do an exegesis of my text. In fact, every time I preach, my first step in preparation is to prepare my exegesis. I work from the exegesis and an open Bible as I work through the truths I want to expose in the sermon. The concept of expository preaching is literally the exposing of the truth in the text. This is prepared by completing a careful exegesis of the texts under consideration. In short, the exposition is built off of the exegesis.

③ Step three is to bridge from the text to the sermon. This bridge looks for the principal theme, central idea, or big idea of the text. You may have preselected your text based upon this principal theme. For example, if you are preaching a series on prayer and select Matthew 6:5–8, you will already know that prayer is the principal theme. If, however, you are preaching through the book of Revelation and come to 4:1–11, you will want to read it repeatedly. By the way, I recommend to my students that they read a passage anywhere from fifteen to twenty-five times as they attempt to identify and isolate the principal theme and main ideas. If, after reading this passage repeatedly, it becomes obvious that the principal theme of this chapter is the worship of the One who sits on the throne of the universe, then this principal theme becomes the subject of the sermon.

---

101 F. B. Huey and Bruce Corley, *A Student's Dictionary for Biblical and Theological Terms* (Grand Rapids: Academic Books, 1983), 76–77.

④   Step four is to outline the sermon in line with the text. As a rule, I follow a sequential order through the text. This is especially true if I am preaching through one of the New Testament epistles. Even the wisdom literature lends itself to this approach.

Sometimes, when I am preaching historical narrative, I will take Mike Yearley's two-stage model approach to the sermon.[102] For example, I recently preached the story of David and Goliath from 1 Samuel 17. I approached the message by retelling the story and then asked the question, "What do we learn from this historical retelling of David's victory over Goliath?" At this point, I shared seven principles that surfaced from the text. Every point was anchored in the Word, surfaced from the Word, and was driven by the Word.

In this preparation stage, you must determine how much exposition you need to give in the sermon. My goal is to attempt to leave no unanswered questions concerning the text's meaning. I want to point out the text's major movements. We will say more about this later.

As I have explained earlier, the way I did my sermon preparation as a senior pastor was to spend all day Monday working through the exegesis of my text(s). My goal was to have both morning and evening sermons prepared. As a rule, I usually worked about twelve hours in preparation on Monday, sometimes longer. What I did not complete on Monday, I finished early on Tuesday.

As I mentioned earlier, at 9:30 on Tuesday morning, I took my outline(s) with me to my worship team meeting. Here, we did three things. First, we critiqued the previous Sunday's sermons start to finish. Second, I taught my sermon(s) in a small group format. We usually averaged about ten to twelve people in the meeting. After I finished teaching my message, I solicited feedback from the team. I looked for suggestions on how to improve, illustrations, and age-graded (stage of life) applications. What would help students? Single adults? Senior adults? The last part was when our musicians would go over the music packages for the three services. For the record, we would set aside special planning days if we were working at packaging a new sermon series. The key here is always lead time and not waiting until the last minute to make plans. Based on the worship team meeting, I would tweak my outlines during the last two hours in the office on Tuesdays and leave them to be typed.

---

102 Mike Yearley, "Connecting Biblical Content with Contemporary Audiences" in Larson and Robinson, 329–32.

⑤   On Wednesday, step five began. I started looking for illustrations. Because of the heaviness of the preaching responsibility, I read a book or more a week and parts of multiple books each week. I also reviewed five to ten magazines and newspapers each week. I was constantly looking for illustrations. I also recruited people to help me as I looked for illustrations. It might interest you to know that Rick Warren has a nine-member research team that assists him weekly in looking for material. Along with my other pastoral responsibilities, I would spend as much time as I could the remainder of the week tweaking the outline and exposition and plugging in illustrations that would help bring the message to life. For the record, it was not unusual for me to still be looking for one more illustration early Sunday morning.

⑥   Step six would also come in to play on Wednesday and Thursday. I begin to nail down the specific applications I would use in the message(s). If I could use application outlines like Rick Warren suggests, I would. I would also alliterate my outlines if I felt like I could do it in just a few minutes. I would not spend an inordinate amount of time working on this. I also tended to keep my outlines flat or linear. I would rather have six points or seven points with no sub points. Why? Sub points get confusing, and my goal was clarity.

⑦   Only after the body of the sermon was done would I work on the introduction, which is step seven. I wanted to make sure that I was introducing what was there so it was prepared at the end of the process. Incidentally, I always recommend to my students that they write out and memorize their introduction so they can begin their sermons making eye contact and full use of gestures. By doing this, the preacher is more apt to gain and keep the listener's attention.

⑧   Step eight is to determine the conclusion. In light of what you have said, what do you want the listeners to know, feel, or do? Although I always tried to tie the conclusion to the main theme and principal point of the message, I usually transitioned into an invitation where we invited people to respond publicly to what they heard. I will elaborate on this further later.

⑨   The transition into the invitation, which is step nine, is always thought through and prayed through carefully. Sometimes I will lead the hearers in a salvation prayer. At other times, I would invite them to come forward and talk with one of our decision counselors. At other times, I used response cards, had people fill them out, and followed up with them the next day. Still at other times, we invited those who wanted to respond to go to the decision counseling room. The point is, I asked them to respond, and I was ready when they did.

(10) The tenth step, which really permeated the entire process, is to pray, depending on the Holy Spirit each step of the way. After all, it is His work, and we are invited to join in.

Additional Issues

Two additional issues I want to address are, first, the notes or no notes question, and second, handouts for notes.

What I teach my students is to take a brief outline with them to the pulpit. It should contain their major points and a few words to trigger recall of illustrations or application points. Primarily I advise this to assist the preacher so that a major idea is not omitted.

I never advise a preacher to take a manuscript to the pulpit because of the temptation to read it, which thoroughly minimizes the connection between the preacher and the congregation. I know that some great preachers have used manuscripts. Jonathan Edwards comes to mind. But I am not sure he could hold sway with a congregation today like he did in his day.

Other homiletics professors argue patently that the preacher not take notes to the pulpit. The argument is primarily to allow the Spirit to lead you as you stand on His Word. That sounds good, but I remember preaching three morning services for a space of seven years, and by the third service I was not sure if I had used an illustration or not. Personally, I needed notes to help keep me on track.

The other issue is that I would always pass out interactive outlines. These would have blanks where key words needed to be added. By doing this, it helped the listeners stay engaged with the message, gave them a map (this is where we start and there is where we finish), and helped them engage in a multi-sensory format. For people with type A personalities, I always put the answers on the back page so they would not miss anything. Some preachers argue that they do not use handouts because it minimizes life-change. I disagree. I will comment on this again.

When I was a small boy, I visited with my Uncle Ralph, who was a missionary with the mission agency originally called the China Inland Mission. He shared an old Chinese proverb with me about the value of writing down what I learned. "Remember this," he said. "The weakest ink is stronger than the strongest mind." His point? Write something down and you have captured it. My point? Write it down and it is yours. I will remind you of this again. I remember going to dinner at my friend Oliver Miles's home right before we left Fort Worth to move to Tennessee. He showed me eight notebooks he had filled up while I was his pastor. No doubt, he captured a lot of what I said.

Much of this chapter we will revisit with much more detail in the following pages. My point here is to urge you to develop a method that works for you and stick with it. As I said earlier, any method is better than no method. Some methods are better than others. Whatever works for you is the best method.

Chapter 10

The Exposition of the Text

With the text selected and the resources in hand, what do you do? Your first task is to do an exegesis of your text from which you can select the appropriate material to expound, or more simply, explain.

In John MacArthur's *Rediscovering Expository Preaching*, he quotes Jay Adams, who said, "Good preaching demands hard work." Adams went on to explain, "I am convinced that the basic reason for poor preaching is the failure to spend adequate time and energy in preparation." His conclusion? "Many preachers—perhaps most—simply don't work long enough on their sermons."[103]

Preliminary Considerations

This being the case, what are some preliminary considerations? If we begin with the end in mind, then we begin with the intent of preparing a thorough exegesis that will form the foundation for the message. Robert Thomas describes the essence of exegesis as "a study of individual words, their backgrounds, their derivation, their usage, their synonyms, their antonyms, their figurative usages, and other lexical aspects." He continues, "Of at least equal, and probably greater, importance is the way words are joined in sentences, paragraphs, sections, etc." He concludes, "A thorough familiarity with the historical background of each book is also imperative."[104] And it is the exegesis we use to prepare our exposition.

---

103 John MacArthur, "A Study Method for Expository Preaching" in John MacArthur, 210.
104 Robert L. Thomas, "Exegesis and Expository Preaching" in MacArthur, 142.

Webster's Dictionary defines "exposition" as 1) a setting forth of the meaning or purpose (as of a writing); 2) a discourse or an example of it designed to convey information or explain what is difficult to understand.[105] In short, exegesis is a tool to get us to our exposition of the text. Stott describes expository preaching thusly:

> It is my contention that all true Christian preaching is expository preaching. Of course if by "expository" sermon is meant a verse-by-verse explanation of a lengthy passage of Scripture, then indeed it is only one possible way of preaching, but this would be a misuse of the word. Properly speaking, "exposition" has a much broader meaning. It refers to the content of the sermon (biblical truth) rather than its style (a running commentary). To expound Scripture is to bring out of the text what is there and expose it to view. The expositor prizes open what appears to be closed, makes plain what is obscure, unravels what is knotted and unfolds what is tightly packed. The opposite of exposition is "imposition," which is to impose on the text what is not there. But the "text" in question could be a verse, or a sentence, or even a single word. It could equally be a paragraph, or a chapter, or a whole book. The size of the text is immaterial, so long as it is biblical. What matters is what we do with it. Whether it is long or short, our responsibility as expositors is to open it up in such a way that it speaks its message clearly, plainly, accurately, relevantly, without addition, subtraction or falsification. In expository preaching the biblical text is neither a conventional introduction to a sermon on a largely different theme, nor a convenient peg on which to hang a ragbag of miscellaneous thoughts, but a master which dictates and controls what is said.[106]

D. A. Carson notes, "Our aim is to take the sacred text, explain what it means, tie it to other Scriptures so people can see the whole a little better, and apply it to life so it bites and heals, instructs and edifies." In effect, this is our aim. This is what we hope to accomplish in our sermon preparation. [107]

---

105 *Webster's Ninth New Collegiate Dictionary*, "exposition."
106 Stott, pp 125–26
107 D.A. Carson, "Teaching the Whole Bible" in Larson and Robinson, 404.

In our preliminary considerations, not only do we need to clarify what we are attempting to accomplish, but we also need to start in prayer. Pray Psalm 119:18, "Open my eyes that I might behold wonderful things from your law." Ask the Lord to help you see what He is saying. As we approach the Word of God, we presuppose a fixed canon and an accurate text. From this, we proceed with our study.

I suggest to my students that they begin by reading their text fifteen to twenty-five times. By doing so, they become familiar with its flow and its nuances, its unique insights and peculiarities. If they are fluent in the biblical languages, I urge them to work in the Hebrew, Aramaic, or Greek text. Then, I suggest that they write their own translation of the text. Robert Thomas notes, "A careful personal translation of the passage to be preached based on thorough exegesis is a primary prerequisite in sermon preparation."[108]

If you are not familiar with the biblical languages, use the best translations in your language coupled with all the linguistic tools at your disposal. Your goal here is to grasp the flow of the text you are studying. John Broadus declares that a preacher "is very guilty before God if he does not honestly strive to understand that which he interprets, and give forth its real meaning and no other."[109]

In the study of the text, we ask three principal questions related to its understanding. What? So what? And now what? Homileticians put this under the categories of investigation, interpretation, and implication. Our exegesis and exposition will focus at first on the initial two questions, so we ask questions about our text. Wiersbe commented, "If I don't talk to my Bible, my Bible isn't likely to talk to me." That is, we must go to the Word with questions—the right questions. [110]

Preliminary Questions

I begin with two preliminary questions concerning the text before me. First, what is the genre? And second, what is the context? The question of genre will determine your hermeneutic approach. David L. Allen points out that genre "means literary category." He suggests four basic categories: narrative, procedural, expository, and hortatory. He adds that narratives tell the great stories of the Bible. Procedural discourses like much of

---

108 Thomas, 149

109 Broadus quoted in Warren Wiersbe, *Preaching and Teaching with Imagination* (Grand Rapids: Baker, 1994), 205.

110 Ibid., 201.

Exodus and Leviticus tell how to accomplish assigned tasks. Expository texts explain. Much of the New Testament epistles reflect this genre. Hortatory texts command and provide directions. Do this, not that. Allen does point out that most of the New Testament epistles are a combination of hortatory and expositional genres. He points out, furthermore, that determining the genre will assist in establishing the correct interpretive approach. [111]

Allen expands his study of genre as he articulates the various specific genres: poetry, proverbs, narrative, parables, and letters (or epistles). Each of these will take a little different approach to interpretation depending on the genre. Another type of genre might include apocalyptic. It is the interpreter's responsibility to determine the genre.[112]

A second preliminary question is, "What is the context?" What precedes and what follow this portion of Scripture? If we are studying the life of David, it is important to know that David was anointed king after God declared to Samuel that He was removing Saul (1 Sam. 15–16). Or when Saul and his sons were slain and their bodies hung on the wall at Beth-shan (1 Sam. 31:10), and news got back to the men of Jabesh-gilead, they traveled all night to retrieve the bodies. Why? Because in 1 Samuel 11, Saul had delivered them from oppression. They felt obligated. We learn this by context. Or consider Jesus' parables of the lost sheep, the lost silver, and the lost son in Luke 15. Context tells us that Jesus was responding to the complaining of the Pharisees and scribes because Jesus "welcomes sinners and eats with them." [113] An old proverb says that a text without a context can be a pretext. Be sure to ask, "What is the context?" As we begin to deal with the text before us, again, questions are in order.

Principal Questions

The question of investigation is "what?" What does it say? Now, we begin to look closer at our text. Start with words and phrases. Is there anything here you do not understand? If you are studying "God's wrath" in Romans 1:18, is the Greek word *orge* or *thumos*? What is the difference? Or if you are studying Mark 8:34–38, what is the difference between the present tense verbs and the aorist tense? Treasures are locked up in words. Are idiomatic expressions being used? For example, what is the significance of Paul's use of the statement, "It [government] does not carry the sword

111 David L. Allen, "The Rules of the Game" in Larson and Robinson, 237.
112 David L. Allen, "Fundamentals of Genre" in Larson and Robinson, 264–67.
113 Luke 15:1–2.

for no reason"? The phrase, "Carry the sword" had a very specific meaning in Roman law.

When Howard Hendricks is teaching hermeneutics and inductive Bible study, he suggests that the student look for things that are emphasized, repeated, related, alike, and unlike. What in this text, he asks, is true to life?[114]

Next, how do words and phrases connect? Are there patterns? Are there comparisons or contrasts? The key here is that as we study the text, we keep asking questions. What does this say?

D. A. Carson raises the issue of "distanciation." He explains this by writing, "Whenever we try to understand the thought of a text, if we are to understand it critically—that is, not in some arbitrary fashion, but with sound reasons, and as the author meant it in the first place—we must first of all grasp the nature and degree of the differences that separate our understanding from the understanding of the text." He concludes, "Only then can we begin to shape our thoughts by the thoughts of the text so we truly understand them." His is an extra word of caution not to rush too quickly past common notions, which may not be as common as one might at first perceive. [115]

MacArthur points out the critical role of observation as we pore over the text and seek to grasp its deeper meaning. He urges the exegete to examine closely the text at hand. Observe carefully, systematically, and persistently![116]

As you study your text, ask the standard research questions: who, what, when, where, why, how, and how much? Keep asking, "What does this text say? What did it say to its original hearers?"

When you begin to think you have exhausted what the text says, then turn to the commentaries to help you grasp further insight.

As you conclude your investigation phase, then move to interpretation phase. The question now is not about what the text says but about what it means. We are looking here for intentions. Here, we move from, "What?" to "So what?"

Perhaps this is an appropriate time to offer commentary on those I call cultural illiterates who take condescending pride in criticizing conservative

---

114 Howard G. Hendricks and William D. Hendricks, *Living By the Book* (Chicago: Moody Press, 1991, 2007), 147–73.

115 D.A. Carson, *Exegetical Fallacies* (Grand Rapids: Baker Academics, 1996), 24.

116 John MacArthur, "A Study Method for Expository Preaching" in MacArthur, 211–12.

Christians for taking the Bible "literally." It is not that we take the Bible literally; it is that we take the Bible seriously. Genre, context, syntax, and language will assist in determining the appropriate meaning. We take the literal literally and the figurative figuratively.

For decades, W. T. Connor taught theology at Southwestern Seminary. He was called the "theologian of the Southwest." He is famous for saying, "The Bible does not mean what it says, it means what it means." Of course, this is a hermeneutical, exegetical, and theological statement. When the Bible says that Christians are "the salt of the earth," it is not saying we are sodium chloride. It is saying that even as salt functions in food, that is the way Christians are to function in the world. When Jesus says you are "my sheep who hear my voice," He is not saying that we are literally sheep. He is speaking in metaphor. You get the point.

When John MacArthur addresses the interpretation issue, he points out that we are trying to create a bridge between gaps that exist between the Bible writers and listeners in the present day.

The first gap is the language gap. The original texts of Scripture were written in Hebrew, Aramaic, and Koine Greek. In order to grasp clearly what the Scripture says and means, we need either a primary understanding of their languages or to have word study assistance. Although I studied years of Hebrew and Greek, I still find *Strong's Exhaustive Concordance,* Rienecker's two-volume *A Linguistic Key to the Greek New Testament,* and A. T. Robertson's *Word Pictures in the New Testament* extremely helpful. [117]

A second gap is the cultural gap. Ancient middle-eastern culture and western culture have few similarities. In fact, there is a great disparity between cultures in the Old Testament and New Testament eras. Like MacArthur, I have found Edersheim's *The Life and Times of Jesus the Messiah* helpful, as well as Barclay's *The Daily Bible Study Series.* I also give a word of caution. Barclay had an anti-supernatural bias, so be cautious with his explanations on the supernatural while using his background material.[118]

A third gap is the geographical gap. A good Bible atlas is extremely helpful. I strongly encourage anyone in the ministry or studying for the ministry to take a tour of Israel and the Holy Land. For me, it made my Bible come alive as I experienced firsthand many of the places where Bible events occurred. [119]

---

117 Ibid., 216–17
118 Ibid.
119 Ibid.

The fourth gap is the historical gap. Understanding the historic context of Bible events often provides insight into the unfolding drama of Scripture. There are multiplicities of works that can provide assistance in the field. I have found the *Holman Bible Dictionary* quite helpful. [120]

So, in the interpretation of Scripture, we are trying to address the issue, not just what the text says, but what the text means. The preacher must study, pray over, think through, and wrestle with the text until he is confident that he grasps both what the text says and what it means. Yet the preacher's goal is not just to come to an understanding of divine truth for himself; his obligation is to so understand it that he might communicate it to his listener. Your goal in this phase of preparation is to help your listeners know what the text says and means.

Even in evangelical Christianity, we find a diversity of opinion (many will say conviction) as to what the Scriptures say and mean. Many fine scholars find themselves on opposite sides of extremely grave issues. I want to challenge you to study the Word of God for yourself and learn to articulate what you believe because you have studied it and wrestled with it on your own. [121]

As you prepare your messages, let me suggest that you take a word of instruction from Wiersbe. In his *Preaching and Teaching with Imagination*, he offers seven questions to ask while preparing your message. Consider what he says.

First, ask, "What does the text say?" This is a repeat of our first principal question. He points out, "The more we mature in ministry, the more we desire to preach the great truths of the Bible and permit the texts to speak for themselves." Here, he is asking those initial information questions about who is writing and to whom. Where and when did this occur? What is the major message? Do I understand the context? Is anything repeated or emphasized here that I should consider especially significant? Are there any metaphors that I can expound upon? He introduces all of this as "factual data."

Second, he asks, "How does the text say it?" He is looking for genre. He does point out, "When the plain sense of Scripture makes good sense, seek no other sense." He highly suggests that the preacher look for word pictures in the text.

His third question concerns "what the text meant to the original hearers." He points out that "what did it mean?" must precede "what does

---

120 Ibid.
121 Carson, *Exegetical*, 15–22

it mean?" At the point in time when this text was penned, how did its first hearers understand its intentions? He points out the value of historical theology as the understanding of how biblical truth has expanded and left significant monuments on the historic and theological landscape. He does remind us that, "The truths of Scripture were revealed gradually and progressively; and as we study the Word, it is important that we know where we are on the road of revelation."[122]

Wiersbe's fourth question asks, "What does the text mean to the Church today?" He points out that it is a necessity for the church to know what it believes, why it believes it, and how it arrived at a particular conclusion. He also points out that whereas there are many secondary issues Christians might disagree about, there is a great body of truth that the vast majority embraces.[123]

As he focuses in, Wiersbe asks fifth, "What does the text mean to me?" He points out that as ministers, we bear witness to what we have seen and heard, and that we have been called to be Christ's ambassadors to a lost world. It is incumbent upon us, therefore, to know what and why we believe and to live what we profess. If we do not live the message as we understand it, we will find it difficult to lead others to do so. As you prepare a message, "Make the text your own!"[124]

The next question is, "What does this text mean to the congregation?" He suggests that the preacher create a grid of a cross section of different people in his congregation and ask himself, "What will this mean to them?"

I got help here from my staff, but if you do not have a staff to assist you, at least you can imagine what the text will mean to various members of your church in the multiple life-stages and circumstances in which they find themselves. Wiersbe's contention is that no matter how much visiting and counseling you do, the best and most effective pastoral ministry is from the pulpit.

The last question is, "How can I make the text meaningful to my hearers?" Here, Wiersbe begins to address the role of imagination. This is a subject we will consider more in a later chapter. It is here that we make the sermon personal. Be aware of Wiersbe's great observation: "Find the place where human life and divine truth meet and there grow your sermon."[125]

---

122 Wiersbe, *Preaching*, 208
123 Ibid., 208–10
124 Ibid., 210–12.
125 Ibid., 307.

As we conclude our thoughts on moving from exegesis to exposition, let me encourage you to embrace these five essentials:

1. Study your text until you know what it says.
2. Study your text until you know what it means.
3. Use Scripture to interpret Scripture.
4. View your text in respect to "progressive revelation."
5. View your text Christologically.

With respect to preaching Christologically yet taking into consideration the necessity of considering the text from the perspective of progressive revelation, we can find both a tension and a failing. The tension comes particularly when the gospel preacher preaches out of the Old Testament. I have heard some pretty good sermons on the principles contained but then find a strange omission of anything about Christ, the failing.

Remember that Luke provides a summary statement concerning Jesus's words to the disciples on the Emmaus Road. "Then beginning with Moses and all the Prophets, He [Jesus] interpreted for them the things concerning Himself in all the Scriptures" (Luke 24:27). Every Old Testament passage can tell us something about Christ.

Over the years, my family has attended services at a Jewish Synagogue or Temple. When the rabbi expounds a passage from the Old Testament, he will not talk about Jesus. As Christian preachers, we should.

Chapter 11

Bridging from Text to Sermon

Bridges permit us to cross from one side to another. For the preacher, crossing from an understanding of the text to the construction of the sermon can be a daunting task. What does this bridge look like?

Once you have completed a thorough exegesis of your text, the next question is, "How do I convey what is in my heart, head, and life into the hearts, heads, and lives of my listeners? How do I organize what I will say?" Before we work through the process, consider first two preliminary issues that I believe deserve attention:

First, some homileticians argue that sermons are more born and not so much constructed. About Ian Pitt-Watson, Darrell Johnson notes:

> He encourages us to think of the crafting of the sermon in terms of the formation of a baby—it is born, not "constructed" as are buildings or airplanes. This is true of any work of human creativity. More often than not, as one does the hard work of preparation, the sermon simply happens, emerging in front of us as we live in the biblical text.[126]

Although the analogy sounds good, I think it is flawed. No sermon simply grows in the spiritual womb without conscious thought of the preacher and suddenly appears fully gestated at the moment of birth. Sermon preparation is hard work and conscious work from start to finish. I choose the word crafted over constructed because there is an art to it all.

---

126 Darrell W. Johnson, *The Glory of Preaching* (Downers Grove: IVP Academics, 2009), 105.

A second preliminary issue is the role of imagination. Contrary to conventional wisdom, this did not begin with the Disney studios. And historically it has been the preacher's ally to pick up on a term introduced by Warren Wiersbe. In fact, Wiersbe states, "Information needs imagination if there is to be communication."[127]

In his first Yale lecture on preaching, Henry Ward Beecher states that imagination is "the most important of all elements that go to make a preacher." Harwood Pattison, who wrote the classic, *The Making of the Sermon*, observes, "It is evident then, that imagination should be pressed into service of the preacher if only for the help which it affords him in making truth vivid."[128]

According to Wiersbe, "Imagination enters into the mind and heart of the biblical writer to think his thoughts and then to communicate those thoughts." He explains, "You can use imagination to see where the needs of people and the text intersect." For those who think that their ability to use imagination has been left behind as they have matured, Wiersbe cites Somerset Maugham, who wrote, "Imagination grows by exercise and contrary to common belief is more powerful in the mature than the young."[129]

My contention is that your ability to craft strong biblical messages from the human perspective will require you to work hard and to use your imagination.

As we move into the tasks surrounding bridging from the text to the sermon, consider the questions that might be raised in order of priority.

Primary Considerations

First, consider the primary considerations as you take your exegesis in hand. What questions need to be asked? You begin by looking at the broad overview of your text. What is the primary theme? Robinson calls this the "Big Idea." Stott calls it the "Dominant Thought." Fasol calls it the "Central Idea of the Text." Charles Simeon calls it the "Proposition." It is all the same thing.

When you consider your text as a whole, what is the one overarching theme? What is the subject you are addressing? Your first task is to identify that one idea.

---

127 Warren Wiersbe, "Imagination: The Preacher's Neglected Ally" in Larson and Robinson, 562.
128 Ibid., 563; Pattison, 257
129 Warren, "Imagination," 564, 566

When Haddon Robinson writes about this "big idea," he provides five characteristics.

He says the idea must be narrow enough to be sharp. Here, you are attempting to answer the question, "What am I talking about?" For example, if you are preaching from Matthew 6:5–15, the subject is prayer.

He maintains, also, that the central idea must have "an expanding force." That means the closer you look and the deeper you dig, the more you find.

Next, he contends that it "must be true," in the sense that "it matters." Why have as the central idea of a text or sermon a subject that does not connect with the life of the listener?

A fourth characteristic is that "it ought to be filled with the realities of life." He explains, "Real theology is how God intersects with our lives and how life looks when we take seriously that the God of the Bible is really there." He stresses that "great sermons go back to the center!"

Finally, he observes what Tom Peters called "the blinding flash of the obvious," that the idea "must be true to God's Word." My definition of truth is "anything and everything that has a one to one correspondence to reality." Does this primary theme or big idea stand true to God's Word?

These then are the five characteristics of a powerful central idea according to Robinson. [130]

Summarizing his approach to developing the big idea, Robinson subdivides it into past and present. What did the biblical writers communicate to the biblical readers? And then he transcends to the present with what he identifies as the "homiletical idea," which he describes as the "idea from Scripture as I phrase it and shape it for the present."[131]

Stott, like Robinson, maintains that "every text has a main theme." That is, each text has "an overriding thrust." As we let the text speak for itself, it is our obligation to let the text identify its main theme. Stott quotes Simeon, who emphasized, "As soon as the subject is chosen, the first enquiry is, 'What is the principal scope and meaning of the text?' Simeon argued, "Reduce your text to a simple proposition, and lay that down as the warp; and then make use of the text itself as the woof ... Screw the word into the minds of your hearers." Stott quotes J. H. Jowett, who declared, "I am convinced that no sermon is ready for preaching ... until we can express its theme in a short, pregnant sentence as clear as crystal."[132]

---

130 Haddon Robinson, "Better Big Ideas" in Larson and Robinson, 353–55. See also Robinson, 33–50.
131 Robinson, "Better," 353–55.
132 Stott, 224–26.

Reinforcing this necessity of starting by identifying the primary theme, John Broadus agrees, stating, "It is important for the sermon to have unity of subject." Broadus explains:

> To state one central idea as the heart of the sermon is not always easy, especially in textual and expository preaching. But the achievement is worth the effort. Even when a text presents several ideas, all of which should be incorporated in the sermon, it is desirable to find for them some bond of unity, some primary idea that will serve as focus or axis or orbit. One may fix attention on one of the ideas as subject and consider the others in relation to it.[133]

John MacArthur notes the value of starting here as he writes, "People love to see the big picture. They want to know how everything fits together." And it starts by identifying the primary theme. What is the text all about? What is the big picture?[134]

F. B. Meyer gives this advice as the preacher attempts to grasp the text's primary theme:

> It only remains to discover the pivot sentence in the next group of verses which you are proposing to treat. That phrase "pivot sentence" is absolutely important. There is in each paragraph one sentence on which it revolves, or a point on which it impinges, like the rocking stones left by the glacier period in balance, as though angels had been playing at a pastime of Herculean feats.

He argues, "In every chapter and paragraph there is such a one."[135]

Meyer continues, saying, "When the pivot-text is chosen it is desirable, so far as possible, to weave into the structure of the sermon all the main points of the surrounding paragraph." He concludes, "There is no absolute law in the matter except one's own sense of the fitness of things."[136]

Next under primary considerations is, "What material do I want to use?" Review your exegesis and decide what is most important. Half of the sermon must be used to explain the biblical content. That means the preacher must be selective in what he chooses and uses. If the task of

---

133 Broadus, 52.

134 MacArthur, "Moving," 292.

135 F.B. Meyer, *Expository Preaching: Plans and Methods* (Grand Rapids: Baker Book House, reprinted 1974), 34–35.

136 Ibid., 35.

expository preaching, and all biblical preaching, as MacArthur maintains, "is to take the mass of raw data from the text and bridge the gap between exegesis and exposition," then the preacher must decide how much of the text and its explanation to use.[137]

Meyer reminds us, "The ministry, therefore, which is most carefully based on Scripture and honours Scripture and saturates itself with Scripture is the ministry which the Spirit of Truth can cooperate with in the most perfect abandonment." He concludes this exhortation, stating:

> All we are advancing now is, that the more carefully we keep to Scripture, the more Scripture there is in our sermons, the more we deal with the whole tenor of the Word of God, the more probable it is that we shall supply the Holy Spirit with those arrows which He knows so well how to use, launching them into the hearts of sinners for their conviction, and the more we shall supply Him with the pure milk of the Word for feeding of babes and the strong meat for the upbuilding of mature character. [138]

In *Lectures to My Students*, Spurgeon records a lecture entitled, "Sermons—Their Matter," in which he reviews the need for sermons to contain strong Bible content. He notes, "The true minister of Christ knows that the true value of a sermon must be, not in its fashion and manner, but in the truth which it contains." He continues, stating, "Whatever else may be present, the absence of edifying, instructive truth, like the absence of flour from bread, will be fatal." He goes on to say, "The discourse should spring out of the text as a rule, and the more evidently it does so the better." [139]

Spurgeon urges upon the preacher, "Brethren, first and above all things, keep to plain evangelical doctrines; whatever else you do or do not preach, be sure incessantly to bring forth the soul-saving truth of Christ and him crucified." He does caution the preacher, "Do not overload a sermon with too much matter." He explains, "All truth is not to be comprised in one discourse." Spurgeon concludes, "Of all I wish to say, this is the sum; my brethren, preach CHRIST, always and ever more. He is the whole gospel. His person, his offices, and work must be our one great, all-comprehending

---

137 MacArthur, "Moving," 289.
138 Meyer, 18–19.
139 Spurgeon, *Lectures*, 70, 72.

theme. The world needs still to be told of its Saviour, and of the way to reach Him."[140]

So I begin by deciding first on the primary theme I will build the sermon around. And next, I am reminded to be diligent to select wisely the biblical content of the message. Coupled with this is the necessity of particularly focusing on the portions of Scripture within the selected text I must work with to persuade my listeners. If the goal of my preaching is to change lives, what truth or truths will I use?

MacArthur argues, "Proper communication in preaching involves taking people through a logical, systematic, and compelling process." I am constantly examining my text to isolate the portion of Scripture that can have the greatest impact on my listeners![141]

Secondary Issues

After I address the primary issues, it is time to move to the next level of questions. Of critical importance as the preacher develops the message is to identify the flow of the text. Whether your text is a chapter, a paragraph, or a verse, it will have a logical flow to it. It is moving. It is going somewhere. Your task is to understand that movement, summarize it, and be able to explain it to your hearers. When MacArthur prepares his messages, one of the first steps for him is to become "aware of the logical flow of the message" because it reflects the logical flow of the text. [142]

As you examine the text, you will need to constantly ask, "What do you my listeners not understand, know, believe, or practice?" What questions are raised from the text? Is there a problem passage where I need to review several interpretations before I communicate which one I believe is most accurate and why? What are the best explanations for this passage? Wiersbe suggests that we use imagination to see where the needs of the people and text intersect. He points out that imagination can help anticipate people's objections and address them. MacArthur urges preachers to "include discussion of problematic interpretations." He states, "Give them hard data." Name the problem, give them the alternatives, and select the best interpretation. [143]

Along this same line of thought, Harry Shields suggests, "From the outset, the listener should be aware that the preacher is seeking to resolve some human dilemma from the perspective of God's Word. At the same

---

140 Ibid., 76–77, 79

141 MacArthur, "Moving," 289.

142 Ibid.

143 Wiersbe, "Imagination," 564; MacArthur, "Moving," 289–90.

time, the preacher will need to anticipate where the resistance will come from the listeners." In fact, he advocates that "the preacher must arrange sermon material with a careful balance between explaining the meaning of the text and answering the questions of the audience."[144]

The preacher, knowing his listeners, needs to ask the question, "From the text, what do I want my listeners to know?" As we move later to application, we will go into more detail, asking what is it that my people need to understand, believe, know, and do.

Although the issues of argument and persuasion will be addressed in the section on application, as the preacher selects his material, he needs to ask, "Is there any truth that I need to press home through argument or persuasion?" Although argument has been somewhat neglected in homiletic studies in recent years, the classic texts on preaching often give attention to the need for its engagement. For example, both Broadus and Pattison give ample space to the place of argument in preaching. In fact, Broadus allocates twenty-eight pages in his classic *On the Preparation and Delivery of Sermons* to the subject. [145]

After Broadus does a thorough review of the place of argument in the preacher's arsenal, he concludes, "As to the style of argument, the chief requisites are, of course, clearness, precision, and force." He explains, "A simple elegance is usually compatible with these." And he notes finally, "And where the subject is exalted and inspiring, and the speaker's whole soul is on fire, some great thunderbolt of argument may blaze with an overpowering splendor."[146]

Likewise, Pattison gives twenty-seven pages to the subject of argument. He points out that "a strain of reasoning ran through the teaching of Jesus." He continues:

> Our faith in the great central truths of salvation rests on a basis of argument. This is emphatically true of the resurrection of our Lord, to which in their preaching the apostles gave such prominence. Faith in the actual resurrection of Jesus rests on the argument from testimony; and faith in the resurrection of the believer rests on the argument from analogy.[147]

---

144 Harry Shields, "Preaching and Spiritual Formation" in Paul Pettit, ed. *Foundations of Spiritual Formation* (Grand Rapids: Kregel Academics, 2008), 263–64.
145 Broadus, 167–95.
146 Ibid., 194–95.
147 Pattison, 225–26.

Pattison recalls the role of Yale President Timothy Dwight in sparking the Second Great Awakening in its eastern manifestation. In Pattison's words, "He turned the tide of fashionable infidelity by his sermons to the students." And much of his sermons constituted the use of argument to lift up Christ and tear down the assumptions and presuppositions of unbelief.[148]

Pattison maintains that every sermon should contain some element of argument; that every sermon should call for some proof and receive it. He may be overstating his case, but we can conclude that certainly there is a place for argument where appropriate. Pattison reminds the preacher to "always keep in view the true end of preaching. This is persuasion. Argument is only a means to an end."[149]

Like Broadus, Pattison reviews the various types of argument: testimony, analogy, cause and effect, effect to cause, and from cumulative evidence. In summarizing the need to develop argumentative ability, Pattison suggests, "Throughout your ministry it will be well that you maintain argumentative studies. Analyze, for example, the arguments of the New Testament. Keep well informed on current theological controversies." He concludes, "Your duty is not so much to preach down error as it is to preach up truth."[150]

My point in including this is that there will be times when you preach that you need to use argument to drive home the truth from the text you have selected. Make sure that the use of argument is one more legitimate tool in your homiletic toolbox.

Tertiary Issues

Before we leave the subject of bridging from the text to the sermon (or moving from the exegesis to selecting the material you will expound upon), three final questions of selection, inclusion, and perspective should be reviewed.

A question the preacher needs to ask again is, "What is the best way to say these truths from my text?" Johnson encourages us to ask, "So what is the best way to say this to the people I know? How now do we package all that we believe we are supposed to preach?" Since we have addressed this previously, it is good that we are reminded of its importance.[151]

---

148 Ibid., 226.
149 Ibid., 227, 229, 232.
150 Ibid., 234–36, 240, 243.
151 Johnson, 128.

Another key consideration is that we need to decide what portion of the text needs additional insight, which the use of cross-referencing may assist. MacArthur points out the importance of connecting the preacher's text with the rest of Scripture. Incidentally, the classic reference work on cross-referencing is *The Library of Scripture Knowledge,* which provides anywhere from five to forty cross-referenced verses for almost every verse in Scripture.[152]

In addressing the importance of using cross-references, MacArthur has this to say:

> By reinforcing the truths of a passage with other Scriptures, you acknowledge the "analogia Scriptura," the analogy of Scripture. This hermeneutic principle states that Scripture does not contradict itself, but is consistent in its teaching. Scripture is its own best interpreter. Obscure passages should always be interpreted in light of clear ones. [153]

Using cross references can assist the preacher in explaining the text before him. Because Scripture is built upon Scripture, two concepts are important. First, when a New Testament passage quotes an Old Testament passage, it is wise to review the latter in order to provide context and understanding. For example, when Ephesians 5:31 references Genesis 2:24, the principle of the sanctity of marriage as God's foundational institution is reinforced.

Also, when the preacher is preaching on a gospel passage, parallel passages provide additional insight into the meaning of the text. If, for example, you are preaching on the story of the rich young ruler from Luke 18:18–23, a cross reference to the parallel passage in Mark 10:17–22 adds insight. In verse 21, the Scripture says, "Then, looking at him, Jesus loved him and said …" The word for love here is the aorist tense of "agape." This helps us to understand Jesus' attitude and intention. It also helps us to understand that the issue here is not that the rich young ruler did not have an effectual call. He made a choice. His net worth had a higher value than the call of God. In effect, he said no to God. Using cross-references can assist in bringing out additional insights. This is also true when working through the entire New Testament.

A final consideration as the preacher is deciding what Bible material to include in his message is the matter of perspective. In fact, imagination

---

152 MacArthur, "Moving," 289.
153 Ibid.

does come into play at this level of decision-making. The question is, "From what perspective will I explain the text?" If I am preaching from Proverbs, will I preach the text from the perspective of Solomon or his son? If I am preaching the story of David and Goliath from 1 Samuel 17, will I tell the story from the perspective of David, Goliath, Eliab, Saul, or a soldier-bystander? If I am preaching the story of Lazarus' resurrection, will I tell it from the perspective of Jesus, Mary, Martha, Lazarus, or a bystander? If I am preaching the parable of the Prodigal Son, will I tell it from the perspective of Jesus, the Prodigal, the father, or the older brother? Or if I am preaching from Ephesians, do I relate the text from Paul's perspective or the perspective of the Ephesian believers? Or if I am preaching from the Pastoral Epistles, do I take Paul's perspective or the perspective of Timothy or Titus? You get the point. As you prepare to preach a passage, the perspective you take can help communicate the old truths in new and receptive ways.

Conclusion

When you prepare your messages, it is of critical importance that you begin by grasping the primary theme of the text. Next, you must select what material you will or will not use. You cannot use it all. It is a matter of prioritizing. You must decide what truths you need to communicate in order to persuade your listeners. You have to grasp the logical flow of your text. You must decide which questions raised in the text merit further explanation. You must decide where the truth of the text intersects with your listeners' needs. You must decide what material to cover and what place argument will play. You have to decide the best way to say these things. You have to choose what cross-references, if any, are necessary. And you select the perspective from which you will communicate the truths in your text. In short, bridging from the text to the sermon is work—hard work. And it is a craft that requires both diligence and imagination.

Meyer summarizes it this way: "It is possible, when expository preaching is rightly practiced, to combine the didactic with the passionate, teaching with intensity, and explanation with appeal." And again we can quote MacArthur, who writes, "Proper communication in preaching involves taking people through a logical, systematic, and compelling process." We cannot take our listeners through a process we have not been through ourselves. Yes, bridging from the text to the sermon is hard work.[154]

---

154 Meyer, 31; MacArthur, "Moving," 289.

Chapter 12

Outlining the Sermon

How many times have you heard or even preached a sermon that seemed to lack a clear-cut pathway? The next step is learning to construct that pathway from point to point.

Once we have worked our way through the text and decided what materials we want to include in our sermon, the next step is organizing our thoughts. Steven Mathewson points out, "The outline stage in sermon preparation is, for some, the most intimidating step in the process." The challenge is to prepare outlines that have substance, communicate clearly, and reflect the flow of the text. This can be a daunting task.[155]

Perhaps it is wise to provide some definitions of an outline. MacArthur identifies the outline as a "roadmap that takes people through the logical flow of a passage to the destination of doctrine to be applied." He points out, "It is critical that this flow be clear." He further explains, "Outline points are hooks to hang thoughts on." He continues, "They are lights along the pathway to enable the listeners to stay on the path." He points out, "They help retain listener attention and facilitate comprehension." He then notes, "An imbalanced, confusing, or complicated outline is self-defeating." I like the idea that the outline is to the sermon what the skeleton is to the body. It provides structure and form.[156]

---

155 Steven D. Mathewson, "Outlines that Work for You, Not Against You" in Larson and Robinson, 361.
156 MacArthur, "Moving" in MacArthur, 289, 295.

Stott points out, "We have labored to isolate the dominant thought. Now we have to knock the material into shape, and particularly into shape as will best serve the dominant thought." As we decide on the material we will use and how it should be organized, Stott notes that we should be "ruthless in discarding the irrelevant," and in contrast, "We should subordinate our material to our theme in such a way as to illumine and enforce it." [157]

According to Hugh Litchfield, the purpose of an outline is "to provide the best possible way to get the controlling idea to come to life in the lives of people." Craddock comments, "No preacher has the right to look for points until he has the point."[158]

Perhaps it is wise to acknowledge that the concept of "points" in a sermon is interchangeable with the "movements" and the "divisions" that other homileticians discuss. In short, it is the way we organize our material in order to communicate its essence. Litchfield points out, "A sermon form is an organizational plan for deciding what kinds of things will be said and done in the sermon and in what sequence."[159]

So the outline serves as a roadmap, as hooks to hang thoughts on, and as a light for our path. It is how we choose to organize the flow of information, insight, and its implications for the listener. That being the case, what are the benefits of a good outline?

Benefits of a Good Outline

So, what are the benefits of a good outline? What differences do they make? Bryan Chapell notes, "A well-planned sermon begins with a good outline which serves as a logical path for the mind." He explains that not only do "good outlines clarify the parts and progress of a sermon in listeners' minds," they also help "crystallize the order and preparation of ideas" in the preacher's mind. He observes that "excellent preaching requires some structure."[160]

A second benefit is that the outline helps the preacher know what he will say. "These are the truths I want my congregation to hear."

---

157 Stott, 228.
158 Hugh Litchfield, "Outlining the Sermon" in Michael Duduit, ed. *Handbook of Contemporary Preaching* (Nashville: Broadman Press, 1992), 163–64.
159 Ibid., 162; McDill, 100; Calvin Miller, 150; *Preaching: The Art of Narrative Exposition* (Grand Rapids: Baker Books, 2006), 150; Litchfield, 168–69.
160 Chapell, 133–34.

It also aids in understanding. According to David Dorsey, "Humans need and appreciate communication that is arranged and organized." McDill points out, "No matter what else the sermon has to commend it, it will likely flounder without the clear and concise outline to follow." Robinson states, "The preacher has the responsibility of helping his congregation think clearly." And he concludes, "A good outline helps with clarity."[161]

Fourth, according to Litchfield, the purpose of the outline is "to provide the best possible way to get the controlling idea to come to life in the lives of people." James Cox opines that "the most important single device for achieving boldness of attack in preaching is a well-constructed outline." [162]

One of the great masters of preaching was Phillips Brooks, who in 1877 wrote:

> In the desire to make a sermon seem free and spontaneous there is a prevalent dislike to giving it its necessary formal structure and organism ... True liberty in writing comes by law, and the more thoroughly the outlines of your work are laid out, the more freely your work will flow, like an unwasted stream between its well-built banks. [163]

In short, Brooks is identifying the benefit of having a clear outline, a formal structure, to the sermon. If there is great benefit to a good outline, what then are the characteristics of a good outline?

Characteristics of a Good Outline

Numerous authors have written on the characteristics of good outlines. In fact, not all writers agree. What is of critical importance to some with certain "rules of thumb" are discarded by others, who see no reason for some qualifications. After surveying the present literature and observing the contemporary scene of preaching, permit me to offer what I consider are the nine most important characteristics of a good outline.

Unity. Chapell includes a good list of characteristics in his *Christ-Centered Preaching*. His first characteristic, reflective of Broadus, is the need for unity. He points out that each point should relate to and

---

161 Johnson, 131; Haddon Robinson, "Clearly: How to Preach So Everyone Understands," in Larson and Robinson, 333.
162 Litchfield, 163
163 McDill, 99.

support the primary theme of the sermon. He counsels the preacher to "eliminate everything that does not contribute directly to the focus of the sermon."[164]

Broadus states, "A work of art may express a variety of ideas, but it cannot remain a work of art unless this variety is held together by the unity of a single idea." He concludes, "The sermon, too, may and should present a variety of thoughts; yet it dare not be a barrage of heterogeneous and arbitrarily assembled elements but must form an organic unity."[165]

Order. A second characteristic of a good outline is its organization; its order. Pascal once said, "Good thoughts are abundant. The art of organizing them is not so common." Broadus explains, "Good order requires first of all that the various ideas comprising the unit of consideration be carefully distinguished from one another; secondly, that they follow one another in true sequence, so making for continuity; and, thirdly, that the order of thought shall move toward a climax."[166]

Proportion. A third characteristic of a good outline is that it has proportion. Some call this symmetry; others call it balance. This is the idea that each point will occupy roughly the same amount of material.

Brevity. Points should be stated concisely. These are pegs to hang thoughts upon. In Chapell's words, "Pegs are not useful if they are nine yards long." MacArthur writes, "I prefer to keep my outlines simple. I do not like complicated ones with a lot of sub-points." McDill points out, "Since a sermon is an oral presentation intended for the ear of the hearer, it is best to keep the outline simple." I concur. In fact, unless the text demands it, I am reluctant even to use sub-points because of the possible confusion.[167]

Harmony. Many homileticians urge that the outline's points (key ideas) should use parallelism in order to demonstrate harmony. This means that each point will match up in order of articles, nouns, verbs, prepositions, and modifiers. MacArthur believes strongly in using a parallel structure.[168]

Clarity. Preachers should work at being clear in what they are saying. Clarity helps the flow of the message stand out. It reinforces the primary theme. The outline, then, should not contain distractions. If it does, do not

---

164 Chapell, 136.
165 Broadus, 97.
166 Ibid., 97–98.
167 Chapell, 136.
168 Ibid., 136–37; MacArthur, "Moving" in MacArthur, 295.

use it. I recall hearing a very prominent preacher expound on the offices of Christ. He stated in his outline that 1) Christ is our Prophet, 2) Christ is our Priest, and 3) Christ is our Potentate. For me, this was a distraction. North Americans do not use potentate. Needless to say, he was not clear to me. And his point seemed contrived with a forced alliteration.

Reflective. By this, I mean that the outline and its points are driven by the text, surface from the text, and are anchored in the text. The outline is not an artificial construct superimposed upon the text. It is reflective of the text.

Movement. The outline should be like signposts in a journey. We start somewhere and we travel to our destination. By movement, I am saying that the outline is progressive and has a destination.

Sequential. I prefer outlines that build one point upon another moving through the text to its climax. Not all sermons require a sequential outline, but if I have a choice, I opt for it. If, for example, I preach a message on five reasons not to worry from Matthew 6:25–34, the points would not necessarily build in sequence, but for me, the message will be stronger if you follow sequentially through your text.

As you work to organize your sermons, let me encourage you to use this checklist to assess your outlines.

Approaches to Organizing and Outlining

In an essay on "Outlining the Sermon" in editor Michael Duduit's anthology, *Handbook of Contemporary Preaching*, Hugh Litchfield identifies thirteen different approaches to outlining sermons. For the sake of brevity and sanity, I will not review all thirteen as options for consideration. I will, however, review several of the more prominent approaches that are popular today.[169]

The one-point sermon is popular today among many preachers. I heard a one-point sermon preached by Jim Cymbala at Thomas Road Baptist Church on Luke 18:40–41, "What do you want me to do for you?" Likewise, I have heard Haddon Robinson preach splendid sermons using one point.

Several years ago, Andy Stanley writing with Lane Jones published *Communicating for a Change*. Their goal in preaching is simply to help people be doers of the Word. Their approach to preaching is to focus on one life-changing principle at a time, one point. They maintain that every sermon should have one idea, message, principle, or truth.[170]

---

169 Litchfield, 169–73.

170 See Andy Stanley and Lane Jones, *Communicating for a Change* (Colorado Springs: Multnomah), 2006.

As Stanley preaches, he uses a "Me, We, God, You, We" outline. In part one he introduces himself and shares the burden or dilemma that he wants to address. Next, "We" provides an attempt to build a relational bridge by looking for common ground. He might say, "This is an issue that all of us must deal with sooner or later." In the "God" portion, he will share the text of Scripture germane to the subject. He cautions that the speaker must avoid the extremes of being either too shallow or too deep in the study of Scripture. In the "You" section, he focuses on applying the message. His philosophy is that everyone can take baby steps moving in the right direction. In the final part, the "We" portion, he uses this as the inspiration moment.

This approach to preaching has worked very well for the North Point Community Church in Atlanta. The caution I have about this approach is that those who listen on a regular basis may not be exposed to enough Scripture preached over the long haul to escape being biblically illiterate. I do believe this is a legitimate concern with reference to this approach to preaching.

Another very popular approach to preaching is the narrative approach. This was first popularized by Professor Fred Craddock at Emory. One of its strongest proponents is Calvin Miller, who wrote *Preaching: The Art of Narrative Exposition*. In a seminal work, an essay entitled "Narrative Preaching," Miller points out that "the narrative sermon, rather than containing stories, is a story which from outset to conclusion, binds the entire sermon to a single plot or theme." He explains, "The theme narrative stays in force all the way through—from the sermon's 'once-upon-a-time' until its 'happily ever after.'"[171]

Although the narrative sermon works well with the historical narrative portions of Scripture, I have found it difficult to utilize in genres that do not lend themselves to story. For example, I would find it a challenge to attempt to use this approach if I were preaching through Psalms or Romans.

A sermon approach that is in some ways a hybrid of the narrative and traditional approaches to outlines is what Michael Yearley identifies as the "two-stage model." His approach is to walk through the chosen text and then to follow it up by suggesting they identify the "life lessons." He explains, "As we go through a passage our main goal is to make sure people can follow the author's train of thought." He explains that they look at the passage then come back to apply the principles identified from the text.[172]

---

171 Calvin Miller, "Narrative Preaching" in Duduit, 103–16.
172 Haddon Robinson, "Set Free from the Cookie Cutter," in Larson and Robinson, 329.

Yearley explains that his approach to preaching is "as if you and I were having a cup of coffee together and talking about the topic of the day, and I have five things I thought were important for you to understand about how to live your life in that area." He further notes that this approach "helps you develop a topic in depth, yet it gives you the ability to talk about five or six different kinds of applications that can hit a variety of people in the congregation." Yearley comments on his approach: "If I were explaining this to the man on the street, would he understand?"[173]

In some ways, Yearley's approach to preaching is somewhat of a throwback to the old Puritan preachers. Reflecting the training of Perkins, they would deal first with the text and its doctrine trying to explain it clearly. Then they would conclude with the application. It does have a history.

These are the approaches that are popular at the beginning of the twenty-first century. I prefer to use more of a traditional approach to sermon presentation and sermon outlines, although I have often used the two-stage model.

Before emulating some of the newer sermon preparation and organization models and discarding the more traditional forms, perhaps it would be wise to consider the words of James Earl Massey:

> Many voices are being raised advising that the old forms and approaches need to be adapted in the interest of greater variety and wider public appeal. There is much to be said for increased appeal and the need to move beyond the limitations of stilted stereotypes ... but when I hear discussions about some sermon form being outmoded I recall something musician Richard Wagner reportedly remarked upon hearing Johannes Brahms play his scintillating Variations and Fuge on a Theme by Handel. Although Wagner was not especially fond of Brahms, he was so moved by the composer's genius that he declared, "That shows what may still be done with the old forms provided someone appears who knows how to treat them."[174]

If the same can be said of preaching, how do we embrace the old forms with respect to outlining and do it well?

---

173 Ibid. 329, 332.
174 Litchfield, 163.

First, we take our selected text and with it the material we desire to communicate. We keep in mind the primary theme of our text and let that serve as a fixed reference point. Stott maintains, "The golden rule for sermon outlines is that each text must be allowed to supply its own structure." Ask yourself, what is the most effective way for me to communicate the truth in this text? Work to grasp the flow of your text. Let the flow, the unfolding of your text, guide your dividing up of the text.[175]

An old adage in leadership studies asks the question, "How do you eat an elephant?" The answer, of course, is, "One bite at a time." So how do you feed your people this text? Give it to them one bite at a time. Our goal is to make sure our listeners are following the author's train of thought. McDougall argues that we need to "find the outline; don't create it." He urges the preacher to "let the passage dictate to you; don't dictate to it." In other words, determine "the outline that best reflects the thought pattern of the author."[176]

A sermon outline I have used many times comes from John 14:1–3. It is my favorite text for funerals.[177] How did I outline it? I ask, "What is the primary theme?" Often, imperative verbs are a clue to what Meyer called "the pivot sentence." Of course, it is Jesus's command, "Let not your heart be troubled." And Jesus provides a three-fold answer. It is when:

1. We put our faith in a person (v. 1). "You believe in God believe also in Me."
2. We put or faith in a place (v. 2a). "In My Father's house are many mansions ..."
3. We put our faith in a promise (vv. 2b–3). "I go to prepare a place for you ... I will come again, and receive you to myself."

Here is an example of an outline that is driven by the text, surfaces from the text, and is anchored in the text. I believe you can do this with every sermon you preach. Notice that it is sequential and has brevity and proportion, among other characteristics.

Some preachers argue that content-related outlines are best. Others plead for application-based outlines. A very fine study of a full range of outline approaches can be found in McDill's *12 Essential Skills for Great Preaching*. He points out from a human perspective, outlines can be

---

175 Stott, 229.
176 Donald G. McDougall, "Central Ideas, Outlines, and Titles" in MacArthur, 233–34.
177 I first read this outline in *The Gospel for the Graveside* by Paul Powell. It is a classic outline.

organized and written with historical statements, propositional statements, application statements, and exhortative statements. He then proceeds a step further and explains how outlines can be God-centered in their approach, following the same four types of statements. His assessment is well worth studying.[178]

Historically, many sermons have been built off longer texts or even multiple texts. In fact, Pattison suggests, "The preacher does well occasionally to draw his text from more than one passage of Scripture." He suggests that some sermons and outlines select texts that corroborate. For example, combine the Second Commandment with Ezekiel 18:19 or consider a charge to a young pastor from Colossians that, like Paul, he is 1) A minister of Jesus Christ (v. 7), 2) A minister of the gospel (v. 23), and 3) A minister of the church (v. 25). These would be considered complementary texts.[179]

Sometimes a sermon might take the approach of tracing a single concept through the Scriptures. For example, Spurgeon preached a masterful sermon on the text, "I have sinned." He then proceeded to show this confession in the lives of Pharaoh, Balaam, Saul, Achan, Judas, Job, and the prodigal. [180]

Although I am confident that the majority of our messages should be the exposition of a single text, I do believe that there are times for an exception. If pure expository preaching is the engagement of a single text, I see this as similar to doing biblical theology where the student studies the theology of a particular book. Periodically, however, systematic theology is in order where a concept is traced through Scripture as its doctrine develops. I do not equate this approach to be identical to "topical" preaching, which selects its "points" with no design or biblical justification.

The primary question is this: does the sermon reflect God's thoughts from God's Word in a disciplined, systematic fashion? If the answer is yes, then it is a biblical sermon. Assuming that the majority of our sermons are the exposition of a single or complementary text, what are some practical guidelines for developing sound outlines?

Guidelines for Developing Good Outlines

I want to conclude by giving you some guidelines for developing good outlines. Please know that seldom will you have your best outline with

178 McDill, 100–07.
179 Pattison, 29–30.
180 Ibid., 31.

one effort. While working on a message, I have often written a dozen or more outlines before I was satisfied with the one I used. Here are some suggestions.

1. Points should not be a restatement of the primary theme. They help support or explain it.
2. Do not let your points stray from the primary theme. Keep them on target.
3. Remember that the main divisions on a sermon serve to amplify, explain, or prove the primary theme.
4. Only sub-divide your points if forced to by the text. Be sparing in your use of sub-points. These can easily get confusing to the listener.
5. Each point should be a complete sentence instead of phrases or single words.
6. Watch out for overlapping points. Make sure that each point is distinct from the others.
7. Strive for balance between points.
8. Make sure that you are following a logical progression of thought.
9. Use statements that can stand alone as universal principles.
10. Strive for contemporary language. Put your points in the present tense.
11. Be cautious with alliteration. If you cannot alliterate it in five minutes, quit trying.
12. Note that quotations of Scripture and illustrations do not constitute points. [181]

---

181 This list is a composite of Litchfield, McDill, and Mathewson's thought.

Chapter 13

The Art of Illustration

Can you imagine what a home would be like if it had no windows? Pretty dark! Or can you conceive of a home with no mirrors? Pretty drab! Illustrations are for sermons what windows and mirrors are for a home.

After I have completed my sermon outline with notes on key thoughts from the text, I walk through and put checks in the margin where I believe an illustration would help bring the text to life. My contention is that illustrations serve two purposes. They function as windows to let light in, and they function as mirrors to help people see themselves and their own spiritual condition. They also serve to inspire and encourage. In short, illustrations ought to illustrate. We most often use illustrations to teach by analogy, clarifying the unknown with the known.

So, after I know the key ideas, main points, explanations, and insights in my sermon, I ask, "Which of these truths need an illustration to help my listeners 'see' what the text is saying?" I choose my illustrations strategically and specifically. Henry Ward Beecher, the great nineteenth-century American pulpiteer, wrote, "He who would hold the ear of the people must either tell stories or paint pictures." This is the principal purpose of illustrations: to make the message come alive. Broadus maintained that "to illustrate ... is to throw light (or luster) upon a subject." Thomas Long explains, "A sermon illustration is like a doorway into a larger room of understanding and experience."[182]

---

182 Broadus, 161, 196; Thomas G. Long, *The Witness of Preaching* (Louisville: Westminster/John Knox Press, 1989), 175.

Other insights come from other writers. Mawhinney explains, "An illustration is an example or a story that helps shed light or clarify truth." Explaining the need for illustrations to clarify, Spurgeon points to Whitefield's testimony, "I use marketplace language." That is, he used language and images that the man on the street could understand. And about D. L. Moody, Spurgeon observes, "Our esteemed brother has a lively, telling style, and he thinks it wise frequently to fasten a nail with the hammer of anecdote."[183]

John MacArthur summarizes the value of illustrations by noting that they make the exposition interesting, memorable, convincing, clear, and motivating. Of course, he primarily adheres to Bible illustrations as his principal method. He does point out, however, the need for preachers to learn to think in analogies and to develop a "parable perspective" in life.[184]

William Sangster, the great British pulpiteer, made this observation about illustrations: "Nothing about true preaching is trifling. That which can clarify the Word of God, and carry conviction to a hesitating mind, that which can banish doubt and remove impediments from frustrated faith is not to be airily set aside by anyone." He said this in response to the notion that although illustrating is subordinate to exposition, it is not a trifling matter.[185]

Sangster asks and answers the question, "What can illustrations do to extend the preacher's power (in the pulpit)?" He suggests that they can help make the message clear, set a congregation at ease, and make the truth impressive. He points out that people are convinced more by what they see than by what they hear and that illustrations help them to see. He goes on to explain that illustrations make preaching interesting and sermons remembered. He also notes that illustrations help persuade people and make repetition possible without weariness. [186]

Spurgeon, like Sangster, also provides a list of the "uses" or benefits of appropriate illustrations. He explains, "We use them, first, to interest the mind and secure the attention of our hearers." He says further, "The use of anecdotes and illustrations render our preaching life-like and vivid." Concerning listeners who are less than sharp, he says, illustrations "may

---

183 Bruce Mawhinney, *Preaching with Freshness* (Grand Rapids: Kregel, 1977), 162; Spurgeon, *Lectures*, 375–76.

184 MacArthur, "Moving" in MacArthur, 292–95.

185 W. E. Sangster, *The Craft of Sermon Illustration* (Grand Rapids: Baker Book House, reprinted 1981), 17.

186 Ibid., 17–20.

be used to explain either doctrines or duties to dull understandings" and continues, "there is a kind of reasoning in anecdotes and illustrations which is very clear to illogical minds." [187]

Spurgeon explains, moreover, that they help the memory grasp and recall the truth. He then relates this story, which helps the student of preaching understand what he is saying:

> What do you remember best in the discourses you heard years ago? I will venture to say that it is some anecdote that the preacher related. It may possibly be some pithy sentence; but it is more probable that it is some striking story which was told in the course of a sermon. Rowland Hill, a little while before he died, was visiting an old friend, who said to him, "Mr. Hill, it is now sixty-five years since I first heard you preach; but I remember your text, and a part of your sermon." "Well," asked the preacher, "what part of the sermon do you recollect?" His friend answered, "You said that some people, when they went to hear a sermon, were very squeamish about the delivery of the preacher. Then you said, 'Supposing you went to hear the will of one of your relatives read and you were expecting a legacy from him; you would hardly think of criticizing the manner in which the lawyer read the will; but you would be all attentive to hear whether anything was left to you, and if so, how much; and that is the way to hear the gospel." Now, the man would not have recollected that for sixty-five years if Mr. Hill had not put the matter in that illustration form ... but, putting the truth in the striking manner that he did, it was remembered for sixty-five years.[188]

Spurgeon concludes his explanation of the illustration's value by pointing out that illustrations frequently arouse feelings and touch emotions. He says, finally, that illustrations catch the ear of the utterly careless. These, maintains Spurgeon, are good reasons for using illustrations. He summarizes by encouraging their use, "The preacher should carry anecdotes and illustrations into the pulpit, and use them as nails to fasten the people's attention to the subject of his sermon." [189]

---

187 Spurgeon, *Lectures*, 378–91.
188 Ibid., 391–92.
189 Ibid., 393–94, 396.

Jesus the Illustrator

One of my preaching professors, Al Fasol, used to encourage his students to use "image level" communication. The consummate illustrator of course was Jesus Himself, and He was the Master at communicating in such a way that people "got it." He communicated in language that was unmistakable.

Long writes, "Jesus came preaching in stories and parables, and when He spoke of the reign of God He often did so in familiar images drawn from ordinary experience." He continues, "Christian preachers ever since have followed Jesus' example and have continued to communicate the gospel through narratives, images, metaphors, and similes drawn from everyday life."[190] So what kinds of communication devices did Jesus employ?

Mawhinney points out that Jesus was a master at using "aphorisms," which is "a short, pointed sentence expressing a truth or precept." Examples of this is where Jesus asked, "What will it profit a man if He gains the whole world and loses his own soul?" or when he stated poignantly, "No man can serve two masters," or when He promised, "Ask and it shall be given to you, seek and you will find; knock and it shall be opened to you." Or who can forget when Jesus said, "Let him who is without sin among you cast the first stone!" Jesus used aphorisms to draw attention to particular truths and mark them with a memorable form.

Coupled with the use of aphorisms, Jesus had a remarkable ability to communicate in language people could understand. He took profound truths and communicated them in simple ways. He was the master of using metaphor and simile.

From agriculture, he talks about how a sower went out to sow. He talks about seed being scattered on a variety of soils. He speaks of putting harvested crops into barns, fig trees, vineyards, and pruning. He relates life to fields and flowers, mother hens and chicks. These are images that most people in first-century Israel would readily understand.

Jesus also speaks about domestic affairs. He talks about building houses and the selection of foundations, household servants and stewards, baking bread, feeding dogs, patching old clothes, and sweeping.

Jesus talks about the world of trade and commerce. He describes buying a field because of costly pearls and hidden treasure. He makes parallels with the spiritual life and money invested, borrowed, or entrusted to others. He discusses creditors and debtors.

---

190 Long, 156.

Jesus uses social situations to describe spiritual and moral truths. He talks of weddings and feasts, judges and widows, beggars, rich men, and the social outcasts, the Samaritans.

He describes political affairs. He speaks of kings going to war and taxes, and alludes to Roman Law, like "going the second mile." He comments on the "eye for an eye" concept of justice.

Jesus uses examples from the marketplace and purchasing food and selling wares. He speaks of the weather. Rain, floods, winds, and the condition of the clouds all find a place in His arsenal of preaching.

Jesus uses the example of children often to help us learn to relate to the Father. Some of His parables, like that of the prodigal son and the good Samaritan, are classics in world literature.

Jesus was a master teacher who communicated on a level that people could understand. If we will study His use of illustrations, we will become more effective communicators. On multiple occasions, He resorts to aphorisms, metaphors, similes, parables, and stories. He used all of these "rhetorical devices" to help communicate the Gospel. He was and is, in effect, God's "Word" to mankind. The wise preacher will learn from the Master and communicate as He did. No wonder it was said of Jesus, "No one ever spoke as He did" and "The multitudes were amazed at His teaching." [191]

Types of Illustrations

The list of various types of illustrations could probably extend indefinitely. For the sake of brevity, I want to share a list of the types of illustrations you will want to consider. Several years ago I wrote a book, *The Way Back Home*, to assist "out of fellowship" Christians relaunch their walks with God. It is built around Jesus's story of the prodigal son. As I wrote it, I included a variety of illustrations. When I subsequently turned the book into a series of sermons, these illustrations were readily available. I want to use this book and the sermons that followed to draw out a list of various types of illustrations. This list is not in some descending hierarchy but rather has been arranged in alphabetical order. I may throw in a few additional illustrations for the sake of balance.

Anecdotes. By definition, this is a short narrative of an interesting, amusing, or biographical incident. Spurgeon and Moody were masters in using the anecdote. In my book, I tell the story (anecdote) of the man who owned a carriage and needed a new carriage driver:

---

191 John 7:46; Matthew 7:28.

He was interviewing prospective drivers for his carriage. He asked each the same question. He told them he was going to have precious cargo. His family would be riding with them. He wanted to ask them something. Down the road was a dangerous drop-off which fell a number of feet. He asked how close to that drop-off they could get before feeling unsafe. The first young man said he probably could get within a foot and a half of it before he would begin to feel uncomfortable. He was told he would not do. The second driver answered that he thought he could get within three feet of the edge before feeling there would be danger to the man's family. He also was told he was not needed. The third man answered that he did not want to find out. He was going to stay as far away from the drop-off as he could. He was hired.

Many times Christians play this game: "How close can I get to sin without neutralizing my effectiveness or forfeiting my fellowship with God, or making a mess out of my life?" It is almost as if we want to go right up to the line. God says do not do that, but stay as far away from it as you can.[192]

Analogies. The definition of an analogy is the resemblance of some particulars between things otherwise unlike: similarity. Analogies are often used to help shed light or insight on the unknown by the known. I point out that the cross is a picture of what God wants to accomplish in our lives: the vertical represents our relationship to God and the horizontal our relationship with other people. I suggest that this is a depiction of God's ultimate intention that we be rightly related to God and our fellow man. I suggest moreover that the horizontal and the vertical meet at the point of forgiveness. The key to a right relationship with God and man is that we experience and express forgiveness.[193]

Behavior Examples. I point out that restlessness can take many forms. "The teenage boy who feels he is missing out and concludes that a little experimentation with drugs will not hurt. The lonely wife addicted to

---

192 Jerry Sutton, *The Way Back Home* (Nashville: B&H, 2002), 70; A good source for learning how to tell anecdotes and stories is Austin Tucker, *The Preacher as Storyteller* (Nashville: B&H), 2008.

193 Sutton, 47.

the escape of an endless parade of soap operas. A weary traveler attracted to secret pornography in a hotel room … In each of these scenarios, the restless heart is enticed toward wanting what God forbids." [194]

Larson suggests that we frequently use examples of everyday disciples. These are stories of how believers follow Christ in the real world. [195]

Bible Stories and References. Many preachers use Bible stories almost exclusively for their illustrative content. I have used the example of David's temptation, Samson's failure, Zaccheus's salvation, Joseph's betrayal, Jesus' preaching of the Sermon on the Mount, and the prayers of Abram, Moses, Joshua, David, Solomon, and on it goes. I recall hearing John MacArthur say once that if you use the Bible for illustrative material, you will never run out. There certainly is a wealth of material in the Word.

Catchphrases. I talk about the Prodigal as having the "grass is greener" syndrome. In another place, I talk about that "no one will ever know" behavior. You can coin phrases describing behavior or aspirations that are memorable to your listeners. [196]

Current Events and Human Interest Stories. I tell the story of the Chernobyl Nuclear Disaster and how bored engineers overrode numerous warnings of "Stop! Dangerous! Go no further!" But each time, the warning was foolishly disregarded. Then I asked, "How often do we refuse to heed God's warnings?" In another place, I use the Apollo 13 disaster as an illustration of how to deal with the unexpected and how they had one opportunity to get home. I use that to describe how God wants us to come home when we are away.[197] I will often take stories from the news headlines to use as illustrations.

Definitions of Words and Concepts, Facts, and Statistics. I define bitterness as "internalized anger." I cite the old adage, "Bitterness does more damage to the vessel in which it is stored than to anyone upon which it is poured." I describe the distinction between joy and happiness. Good sermons help clarify understanding. Definitions establish limits and explain differences and similarities. [198]

Fables. I like using Aesop's Fables as a source of illustrations. I particularly like the one about the dog on the manger. He was not going

---

194 Ibid., 6.
195 Craig Brian Larson, "Power of Everyday-Disciple Illustrations" in Larson and Robinson, 530–31.
196 Sutton 6, 12.
197 Ibid., 6, 25.
198 Ibid., 48; Haddon Robinson, *Biblical Preaching: The Development and Delivery of Expository Messages*, 2nd ed. (Grand Rapids: Baker Academic, 2008), 142.

to eat any hay, but he was not going to let the other animals eat it either. Some people are like that!

Figures of Speech: Metaphors and Similes. A simile is a comparison using "like" or "as." A metaphor is a simple comparison. "As the deer pants after the water brook, so my heart pants after you Oh God" is a simile. "I am the vine. You are the branches" is a metaphor. In our culture, these figures of speech connect. In teaching the disciplines of rhetoric, Aristotle once said, "The greatest thing by far was to be master of the metaphor."[199]

Hymns, poems, musical lyrics. In one place, I quote an old poem/ hymn penned by John Newton, "Thou art coming to a King, Large petitions with thee bring, for His grace and power are such, None can ever ask too much." Or consider this old poem:

How Thou canst think so well of us,
> And be the Good Thou art,
> Is darkness to my intellect,
> But sunshine to my heart.

Or consider this poem by an unknown author:

> The clock of life is wound but once,
> And no man has the power,
> To tell just when the hands will stop,
> At late or early hour.
> Now is the only time we own;
> Give, love, toil with a will,
> And place no faith in tomorrow,
> For the clock may then be still.

Lyrics well placed still connect. [200]

Journal Articles. For avid readers, journals can often provide essays and articles with interesting stories ripe for picking.

Media: Movies, Television, and Radio. The media is the language of the day. If you tell a story or quote from a movie, I suggest you make sure the movie is clean. Otherwise, your efforts at relevance may be misinterpreted as compromising and become a distraction. Here is where it is important to know your congregation.

Narration. Retelling a Bible narrative from a first-person perspective or from the vantage point of a bystander can shed new light on old truths.

---

199 Mawhinney, 189.
200 Sutton, 72, 40, 77.

Max Lucado is a master of retelling in narrative form some of the old stories from the Bible. How would the story of the resurrection sound, for example, from Peter's perspective. How did he see it? Experience it? How did it impact him? What emotional roller coaster did he travel? Robinson points out:

> Narration means communicating with imagination, and imagination reflects the insights of faith, imagination is the half brother to interpretation because both relate to the text. In interpretation, we determine what the passage means from what the passage says. In the same way, imagination goes one step beyond the biblical facts and yet stays tied to it. [201]

Newspapers, Magazines, Books, Websites, and Emails. The print media is a goldmine of illustrative material. I must confess, I have a passion for books and find them filled with a great array of illustrative material. When I was a pastor, it was not unusual for me to spend five hours a week in Barnes and Noble looking at books, magazines, and newspapers. I was always looking for material to use in sermon preparation. I usually used three newspapers a week for sermon prep and would often buy one or more magazines a week. I had five or six websites I had marked favorites. Periodically people would email me a great story to use as an illustration. I will say this again, but if a story seems too good to be true, it probably is. Always verify your facts.

It was not unusual for me to quote a letter to the editor or a "Dear Abby" column. Oftentimes I would use something from the newspaper or a popular book to introduce an issue. When preaching about the power of God to restore, I introduced it with a citation from Harold Kushner's *Why Bad Things Happen to Good People* and his contention that God, after all, is not all powerful. Sometimes a negative example can get our listeners' attention.[202]

Parables. In layman's terms, a parable is an earthly story with a heavenly meaning. In Matthew 7:24–27, we have the parable of two builders. One built his house on sand, the other on rock. Or recall Nathan telling David the story of the man with the lamb that was taken by a more powerful man in 2 Samuel 12. With a bit of imagination, we can even write our own parables.

---

201 Robinson, 151.
202 Sutton, 49, 57.

Sangster points out, "Men are on guard against denunciation but nobody ever guarded himself against a clean storyteller. The seemingly innocent tale guides into the mind unhindered and on the lips of a master it needs no explanation. To moralize is quite unnecessary. The tale ends and conscience stabs from within."[203]

Personal Stories. When I was in seminary, I was told to limit personal stories. I believe that advice was wrong. Human interest stories, particularly yours, will hold the interest of your listeners. I have told stories about my dogs, my family, my girls, my wife, growing up, educational experiences, and work experiences. Here is one example:

> One of my mentors was a professor of evangelism named Oscar Thompson. In the late 1970s I graded for him and as a result was given some quality time with this precious man of God. During those days I watched him slowly die of a very painful bone cancer. I can recall sitting in his office. As tears streamed down his face, he confessed that he felt like his foot was in a bucket of fire. His pain was excruciating. Yet, at the very same time, he related to me he had an incredible joy knowing that both his life and circumstances were in the hands of his loving Heavenly Father. He was one man, I am convinced, who had discovered the secret of joy.[204]

Quotations. Robinson points out that quotations are often used to punctuate or add authority to an idea. He observes, "Anchoring a point with some wording that digs into the mind is probably the major reason preachers turn to quotations in sermons." He points out that as a rule of thumb, quotes should be brief. [205]

Here are some quotes that I have used in order to give you the flavor of what is effective.

Satan, like a fisher, baits his hook according to the appetite of the fish.
—Thomas Adams

To walk out of God's will is to step into nowhere.
—C. S. Lewis

---

203 Sangster, 33.
204 Sutton, 55.
205 Robinson, 146, 148.

The Lord has a golden scepter and an iron rod. Those who will not bow
to one, shall be broken by the other.
—Thomas Watson

Let the quantity of thy sins be the measure of thy repentance.
—Isaac Bargrave

You cannot repent too soon because you do not know how soon it will
be too late.
—Thomas Fuller

God loves each of us as if there were only one of us.
—Augustine

The truth about man is that he needs to be loved the most when he
deserves it the least.
—Author Unknown

Joy is the serious business of Heaven.
—C. S. Lewis

It costs to follow Jesus Christ, but it costs more not to.
—Author Unknown

The loneliest place in the world is the human heart when love is absent.
—E. C. McKenzie

Love is not a feeling but a choice.
—Soren Kierkegaard[206]

Restatement or Reiteration. This makes a concept clear either by
restating it again or by stating it again but using different wording. This
impresses ideas on people's minds. [207]

Sports Stories. With the world's love for sports, a good sports story
will often catch people's attention. I must confess that I am an avid baseball
fan, and I tell my students that my one overt character flaw is that I am a
diehard Yankee fan. Here are a couple of illustrations I have used.

I love the story told by George Will. It seems that Babe Ruth was at bat
while Umpire Babe Pinelli called balls and strikes from behind the plate.
The pitcher gets his signal, rocks, and fires. Ruth swings and misses. "Strike

---

206Sutton, 5, 9, 13, 29, 40, 45, 53, 61, 73.
207 Robinson, 140.

one," Pinelli yells. The Babe steps back in. The pitch is delivered and again Ruth takes a mighty swing … and misses. "Strike two," says Pinelli. With that, Babe Ruth digs in for the next pitch. The pitcher winds up and delivers. Ruth does not move. From behind home plate Pinelli cries, "Strike three, the batter's out." Babe Ruth gets in Pinelli's face and says, "There's forty thousand people here who know that last one was a ball, tomato head." Pinelli looks around at the stadium full of people and then looks back to Ruth. "Maybe so," he says, "but mine is the only opinion that counts. The batter's out!" Similar to Babe Pinelli, God's opinion is the only one that matters. [208]

I love to tell the folks I preach to that it does not matter where you are but the direction in which you are moving that counts. Anyone can start with God right now. And anyone can start over with God right now. It was one of the most embarrassing losses in Yankee history. On May 15, 1941, the Yanks were demolished 13–1 by Chicago behind the brilliant pitching of Edgar Smith. No bright spots in that day of hometown humiliation! There was one statistic of note, however. That day Joe DiMaggio got a single hit. Nothing to write home about! Yet every game for the next fifty-six games DiMaggio got a hit. By the time he completed his run, he set a fifty-six game hitting streak record that will in all likelihood never be broken. The day of one of his worst defeats actually began the season of his greatest victory. The same can be true of you. No matter where you are today, no matter how defeated you might be, this could be the beginning of your life's greatest season of accomplishment and achievement. After all, it is not how you start but how you finish that matters.

Like I said, there are plenty of illustrations in the world of sports.

Stories from History. If you are a lover of history, and I am, you will have no shortage of stories from the pages of history that might illustrate the subjects about which you are preaching. Here is an example.

> Does the name Raynald ring a bell? Probably not. Actually, he was Raynald III, a fourteenth-century duke in an area that is now modern-day Belgium. Raynald loved to eat and was grotesquely overweight. As the story goes, there was a revolt in the kingdom led by Raynald's younger brother. In custody, Raynald had a prison cell built around him. The room had no bars on the windows. It did not even have a lock on the door, which was built slightly smaller than normal.

---

208 Sutton., 44.

The younger brother chided Raynald, informing him that at any time he chose, he could come out and receive his crown and his position back. All Raynald had to do was go on a self-enforced diet, walk out, and claim his throne. His brother even offered to restore his title and wealth as soon as he left the room.

Yet, the younger brother knew Raynald's weakness. He loved food. So each day the younger brother had delivered to the elder a sumptuous variety of delicacies. And Raynald continued to gain weight, a prisoner, not of locks and bars, but of his own appetite. What Raynald would never do was disengage from his appetite, which the apostle John identifies as an integral part of living "in the world."[209]

Any appetites got you locked up?

This is a selection of the various types of illustrations I suggest you use. These connect well with listeners. Yet, now, the question is, "How do I cultivate sermon illustrations?" How can I be more adept at illustrative ability?

Cultivating Your Illustrative Ability

I believe that anyone with a desire and a willingness to work can improve his or her ability to illustrate well. Permit me to give you five suggestions that if implemented can assist you in your ability to cultivate illustrations.

First, cultivate your ability of observation. Broadus, quoting one of the Beechers, said he had learned to "keep his eyes and ears open." Always and everywhere be asking yourself, "Is there anything I am observing that I can use as an illustration?" Discipline yourself to see. If you see hairstylists, the first thing they look at is your hair. If you meet shoe salesmen, they look at your shoes. A car salesman wants to know what kind of car you drive.[210]

Preachers should have a biblical fixation. Whenever they meet someone, they should think, "What is this person's spiritual condition?" And about events around them, "Is there anything here that illustrates what I am preaching on?" Sangster points out, "Illustrations crowd upon us every day. The alert, sensitive, disciplined mind just takes them in." [211]

---

209 Ibid., 36–37.
210 Broadus, 200.
211 Sangster, 49.

Second, cultivate your abilities of imagination. Some of your best illustrations may be a story you created or perhaps the way you saw or described something everyone else sees, just not viewed the same way. To improve in this area, let me suggest you read and implement Warren Wiersbe's *Preaching and Teaching with Imagination.* Jesus, no doubt, was a master at this. Sangster observes, "If he [the preacher looking for illustrations] educates his intuition for illustrations, he need never look for them. They will look for him." [212]

Third, cultivate your abilities of investigation. Wayne McDill does an insightful job at encouraging students to cultivate the ability to identify "natural analogies." He maintains, "There is a parallel picture in human experience for every concept God intends to make known to man." He explains:

> Natural analogies are relationships, circumstances, events, or other factors observed in the natural dimension that may serve as parallel images for theological concepts. These are analogous, having points of likeness that make them useful in better understanding, visualizing, accepting, and preaching biblical concepts. They are natural, and familiar parts of the human experience.[213]

McDill urges, "We declare spiritual truth clothed in earthly images." How can this be done? He suggests that we begin with a clear idea of what we want to explain and that we next generalize the concept. That is, we identify the concept, principle, or idea we want to shed light upon. For example, Matthew 9:35–37 talks about the lack of laborers for God's harvest. The general concept is, "We need to see the need." Next, he suggests we look and brainstorm for natural analogies, looking for examples in the world around us. Finally, he concludes that we select the best and use it. This simple process can easily guide our search for illustrations.

Fourth, cultivate your abilities of preservation. Mawhinney points out, "Illustrations, like babies, have a habit of being born at awkward times." Like my own practice, he suggests that preachers get in the habit of carrying a notebook or utilizing some method to capture illustrations when you see them. Sangster points out, "However good your natural memory, you note it in pen and ink" and it is captured. If you think it

---

212 Ibid., 52.
213 McDill, 141–42.

might become an illustration, record it. Sometimes I will send myself an email on my Blackberry.[214]

And fifth, cultivate your abilities at deliberation. Wait until you have outlined your sermon and know exactly what it is that needs illustrating. Prematurely injecting illustrations often leads to an awkward illustration that confuses instead of clarifies.

Cautions When Illustrating

Before concluding this chapter with some practical guidelines about using illustrations, it is probably wise to express some cautions that have been expressed by some of the great preachers. Broadus cautions preachers not to use every illustration that occurs to them. He also urges preachers to use a variety of different types of illustrations. Finally, he advises preachers not to introduce an illustration, "Now let me illustrate," but simply do it. Sangster adds to this advice by warning preachers not to make a rule that every sermon will have a certain number of illustrations. Only illustrate where they are necessary and appropriate.[215]

In *The Art and Craft of Biblical Preaching*, Wayne Harvey writes a wonderful article, "Seven Questions for Staying above Reproach." He points out that "using inaccurate or untrue illustrations can threaten our integrity (and credibility)." He then provides a checklist to help the preacher maintain healthy illustrations. Here are his questions:

1. "Am I inserting myself into someone else's illustration?" Do not say something happened to you if it did not.
2. In the illustration, do you describe someone as "a member of your former church?" This is problematic. Just say "I once knew someone who …"
3. "Should this illustration be checked for accuracy?" As I have said before, if it sounds too good to be true, it probably is.
4. "Will this illustration be sensitive to people in the congregation?" Terms like "little old lady" may be offensive.
5. "Will this particular congregation relate to the illustration?" He points out that every church is different.
6. "Is this illustration too detailed?" Remember, impact comes from relevant details.

---

214 Ibid., 142–48.
215 Mawhinney, 166.

7. "Am I clearly differentiating (between) true and imaginative stories?" He seriously cautions that telling half-true or untrue stories to our congregations can threaten our integrity. [216]

Permit me to add two additional cautions. First, never violate a confidence by telling that confidence as an illustration. That can actually carry a liability. Leave confidences buried! Second, never speak of your wife or children in a negative manner. I recall a very popular preacher describe something his son did that was "dumb." I cringe to this day wondering if the laugh at the son's expense left any emotional scars. Never say anything negative about your family. If you need humor from your family, use self-deprecating humor about yourself.

Final Guidelines for Illustrating

Permit me to give you some final guidelines for illustrating. This list is the collective wisdom of many great pulpiteers. [217]

1. If you cannot illustrate it, do not preach it.
2. Illustrations are everywhere, so keep your eyes open.
3. Create a method for saving illustrations that works for you.
4. Do not waste a good illustration. Save it for an opportune time.
5. The introduction and the conclusion of the message are the two most strategic places for illustrations.
6. The best illustrations are usually shorter illustrations.
7. If a personal story is not yours, give credit, but do not go overboard.
8. Share illustrations with other preachers. The supply of good illustrations is virtually endless.
9. Do not forget that people remember your illustrations longer than they remember the sermon as a whole.
10. Make sure that an illustration from history is accurate. Check your facts. If you do not, you may be embarrassed by someone who does.
11. Be careful with Bible illustrations. Some people, like Jay Adams, say never use Bible illustrations. Others, like MacArthur, say use them first.

---

216 Wayne Harvey, "Illustrating with Integrity and Sensitivity" in Larson and Robinson, 521–24.
217 Stephen Brown, "Illustrating the Sermon," in Duduit, 204–07; Larson, "The Power," in Larson and Robinson, 530–31; Robinson 153–57.

12. Make sure that your illustrations are appropriate to the congregation to which they are given.
13. Write the body of your sermon before illustrating it in order to make sure the illustrations fit.
14. In illustrations, help people see obedience in action.
15. Be specific in illustrations.
16. The best illustrations address both the mind and the emotions of the listener.
17. Remember that the most powerful illustrations are personal examples and experiences.
18. Get help in looking for illustrations. Many people in your church would love to help you if you provide them with some lead time and guidelines on what to look for. Over the years, many wonderful people have helped me look for illustrations. And I am grateful to each one.

As we draw our study of illustrating to a conclusion, let me leave you with Sangster's parting words:

> Yet, at the last, preaching is not just religious speaking; not the art of making a sermon and delivering it, but rather making a preacher and delivering Christ through him. Therefore, it will not be resented if I remind my readers in parting from them that our most impressive illustration in the end is ourselves. [218]

---

218 Sangster, 118.

Chapter 14

Application in the Sermon

The only people who like change are babies with wet diapers. Yet facilitating change is the one great purpose of preaching. So, what steps do we take to help facilitate change in the lives of our listeners?

After the preacher has the body of the sermon prepared and selected appropriate illustrations to help it come alive, the last task on the body of the sermon is to identify and clarify the application. I reserve this task for last, other than preparing the introduction and conclusion, so that the preacher has ample time to think, mediate, and pray over the text. If our ultimate goal is not simply to transfer information but to facilitate transformation, this is the most critical part of the preparation process.

Harry Emerson Fosdick once said notably, "The purpose of preaching is not to explain a subject, but to achieve an object." In short, the goal is not information but transformation. John MacArthur puts it this way:

> Truly biblical preaching must be both didactic and practical. The two things are not opposed to one another. They are, however, notoriously difficult to keep in balance. Those who stress sound doctrine sometimes neglect the passion and pleading that are necessary parts of biblical preaching (2 Corinthians 5:11, 20; Luke 14:23). And those who stress practical matters too often neglect to build a foundation of sound doctrine.

So, the biblical preacher must communicate truth for the purpose of transformation.[219]

The classic statement from John Broadus tells us, "Application, in the strict sense, is that part, or those parts, of the discourse in which we show how the subject applies to the persons addressed, what practical instructions it offers them, what practical demands it makes upon them." In commenting on the component parts of the sermon, Broadus remarks, "if illustration is the servant of all, then application is the master of all."[220]

Assumptions

Before examining the details of applications, it is wise to first consider some assumptions related to this discipline. It almost goes without saying that the preacher should live out what he proclaims. Miller points out, "Application is the place at which the preacher leverages the strongest influence." As such, "The riskiest single sentence that appears in the sermon is, 'Here is what you do with what I have just told you.'" Here, the preacher's credibility is on the line.[221]

It should be noted that without application, the sermon is not a sermon; it is just a talk or a lecture. Miller notes, "Without application there is no sermon." He insists, "Sermons must take the information they dispense and tell the church what to do with it." That is, "Every sermon we preach should bring the listener to the point of responsibility for doing the will of Christ."[222]

Describing the task of incorporating application in the sermon, Broadus observes, "Preaching is essentially personal encounter, in which the preacher's will is making a claim through the truth upon the will of the hearer. If there is no summons, there is no sermon." [223]

Fabarez points out that if a subject is "right to preach, then it is right for the preacher to live it out." He cites Richard Baxter's *The Reformed Pastor* where Baxter urged pastors to "be careful ... that you preach to yourselves the sermons which you study, before you preach them to others. If you did this for your own sakes, it would not be lost labor; but if I am

---

219 Warren Wiersbe, "Imagination: The Preacher's Neglected Ally," in Larson and Robinson, 563; Michael Fabarez, *Preaching that Changes Lives* (Eugene: Wipf and Stock Publishers, 2002), IX.
220 Broadus, 211, 210.
221 Miller, *Preaching*, 80.
222 Ibid., 79, 88.
223 Broadus, 210.

speaking to you upon the public account, that would do it for the sake of the church."[224]

I am reminded of a statement in the classic sermon by Gilbert Tennent, "The Danger of an Unconverted Ministry." Preached during the First Great Awakening in 1740, he addressed the issue of preachers who were not themselves converted. He asked, "Isn't an unconverted minister like a man who would learn others to swim, before he has learn'd it himself, and so is drowned in the act, and dies like a fool?"[225]

It is imperative that the preacher live out what he preaches! In Ezra 7:10, we read, "For Ezra had prepared his heart to seek the law of the Lord, and to do it, and to teach statutes and ordinances in Israel." The preacher should emulate Ezra's example.[226]

Sadly, Chapell points out, "Surveys find little difference … when comparing the behavior of … born again Christians before and after their conversion experience." He points out, "Faith can remain abstract idealism for too many." Observing the sad state of affairs in too many churches, he maintains, "Without application, a preacher has no reason to preach, because truth without actual or potential application fulfills no redemptive purpose." Then, he concludes, "This means that at its heart preaching is not merely the proclamation of truth but truth applied."[227]

Having said that, we should be reminded that "Jesus' goal in preaching was to produce a 'life-changing' experience." To Him, an effective sermon resulted in people grasping truth and putting it into action. Changing lives is always the goal of biblical preaching![228]

Before we get into the heart of our study on application, perhaps it would be appropriate to consider an objection to the notion that application is a legitimate portion of the sermon. Darrell Johnson, in his impressive *The Glory of Preaching*, argues that preachers should communicate the text's "implications" instead of using the term "application." He argues, "No one but the Lord can apply the text." He concludes, "To expect preachers to apply the text for their listeners is to ask them to play God." He argues, "The pressure to apply is a modernist pressure, not a biblical pressure."[229]

---

224 Fabarez, 27.

225 Richard Bushman, ed. *The Great Awakening: Documents of the Revival of Religion: 1740–1745* (New York: Atheneum, 1970), 91.

226 Fabrez, 27.

227 Chapell, 209–10

228 Fabarez , XI.

229 Johnson, 158–59.

Johnson offers for an example Peter's Acts 2 Pentecost sermon and points out that by the proclamation of truth, the listeners were "pierced to the heart." He then observes that the people cried out, "What shall we do?" (Acts 2:37). He concludes, "The burden of 'doing something' about what was preached did not lie with Peter." He explains, "The Spirit through the Word brought about a piercing conviction, causing hearts to cry out, 'What shall we do?'" His argument is that the Spirit is responsible for making the application of the Word.[230]

Providing a personal example from his mission and preaching days in the Philippines, he relates that he read his text during a critical time in the life of the country and "let the Spirit make the application." He concluded, "I saw the Lord of the text Himself work out the implications of the text. I did not have to come up with any application." [231]

From his understanding of Acts 2 and his personal example, his conclusion is this:

> Does that mean that we are not to give any word of exhortation, any imperative, any concrete steps to take? No. For many texts do exactly that. It is just that we are to give any such imperative, any steps to take, in the context of the text's own inherent implications.[232]

Johnson concludes his investigation on the subject we call application with these words:

> The question, therefore, is not "How should we apply the Word?" The question is "Where is the Word leading us?" and "Will we cooperate and enter in?" The question is not "What do I the preacher want people to do as a result of hearing this word?" The question is not even, "What do I want to see happen in people's lives as a result of hearing the word?" The question is "What do I want to see God do as a result of people hearing the word?" Even better, "What does God want to do?" [233]

So, how do we assess Johnson's assertions? First, and this is obvious, this is the outworking of his own theological presuppositions. And as one of my seminary professors once said, "Your presuppositions dictate

---

230 Ibid.,160–61.
231 Ibid., 163.
232 Ibid., 163.
233 Ibid., 165.

your conclusions." Second, if he is cautioning the preacher not to say what the Scripture does not say, his is a legitimate concern. Noting that, Peter's response in Acts 2:38 is the application of verse 37's heart cry of the listeners. Peter made application. Moreover, when Paul states in 2 Corinthians 5:11, "knowing the terror of the Lord, we persuade men," he is saying that the preacher is responsible for persuading and applying the text. And finally, if we consider 2 Timothy 4:2 as normative, where Paul exhorted Timothy to "preach the Word; be ready in season and out of season; reprove, rebuke, exhort, with great patience and instruction," then we cannot come to any other conclusion than that the preacher is obligated to make application of the text he is preaching. And the fact that Johnson did not draw an application in his Manila sermon demonstrates that the Spirit can make the application even if we fail to do so. It does not mean that we ought not make the application. Personally, I do not think Johnson made his case.

In attempting to provide a framework around which our study of the discipline of application can be readily embraced, it might be well to consider the words of Haddon Robinson. He admonishes the preacher to "give as much biblical information as the people need to understand the passage, and no more. Then move to the application." But make sure that your listeners understand the biblical information. Citing Spurgeon, Robinson says, "The people in the marketplace cannot learn the language of the academy, so the people of the academy must learn the language of the marketplace. It's the pastor's job to translate."[234]

Before getting into the details of application, it is appropriate to point out that the biblical truth and its application are not identical. The biblical truth or biblical principle is constant. The application can change with the times and circumstances. Perhaps it is wise to remind the preacher of a truth from Robinson's experience. "Life-changing preaching does not talk to the people about the Bible. Instead, it talks to the people about themselves—their questions, hurts, fears, and struggles—from the Bible."[235]

Disciplines in Application

One of Jesus' parting instructions to His apostles and to the church is that we teach disciples to "observe whatever I have commanded you." The exhortation from Matthew 28:20 is one of practice of doing what He

---

234 Haddon Robinson, "Blending Bible Content and Life Application," in Larson and Robinson, 295–96.
235 Ibid., 299.

said. Application is the communicating of the answers to the "So What?" and "Now What?" questions. In light of what this text says and means, what am I the listener supposed to do in response to it? Chapell points out that application should be specific and that taking that course will require courage. We are attempting to answer the question, "What does God want us to do as a result of hearing this message?" In Timothy Warren's words, "The expositional preaching process is not completed until God's people think and act differently for having heard the Word expounded ... for its goal is to manifest or reveal God's truth by living it out."[236]

According to David Veerman, "Application focuses the truth of God's Word on specific, life-related situations. It helps people know what to do or how to use what they have learned. Application persuades people to act." He goes on to say that for application to hit home, it must start with the needs of the listeners. He suggests that the three categories of needs are felt needs, hidden needs, and spiritual needs.[237]

To clarify what application is, perhaps it would be appropriate to note what it is not. Veerman points out that it is not additional information, not just understanding the truth, not simply being relevant, and not just explaining how someone else might have handled a similar situation. These might prepare for application but in and of themselves are not application.[238]

Why is it, then, that implementing effective application is so difficult? Veerman, again, provides some insight. First, he suggests that it is hard work. It is not easy to assist people to ask the right questions or motivate people to action. Next, he observes that often preachers begin with wrong assumptions. Specifically, he states don't assume that people will make a connection between the lesson and their lives. The next reason is simply fear—perhaps the fear of being too simplistic. He notes that people are waiting for "a life-changing challenge!" And finally, he suggests that many preachers have just not been trained to identify and utilize application in their preaching. [239]

So why, then, is application important? Simply put, it is important because the goal of preaching, like the goal of the Bible, is that people might change or more accurately be changed. The Bible is replete with the message of change.

---

236 Ibid., 292; Fabarez 19.
237 David Veerman, "Apply Within," in Larson and Robinson, 285–86, 288.
238 Ibid., 285.
239 Ibid., 284–85

Romans 12:2—"Be not conformed to this world but be transformed by the renewing of your mind."

Galatians 4:19—"My children, with whom I am again in travail until Christ is formed in you."

Ephesians 4:15—"We are to grow up in all aspects unto Him ..."

Ephesians 4:22—"Lay aside the old self ... and be renewed in the spirit of your minds."

Colossians 1:27—"Christ in you the hope of glory ..."

Colossians 1:28—"That we may present every man complete in Christ."

Colossians 2:6–7—"As you therefore received Christ Jesus the Lord, so walk in Him having been rooted and now being built up in Him and established in your faith."

Taken collectively, these venues have one common thread. God's desire is that we should grow from spiritual depravity to spiritual maturity. And it is the application of the Word of God that enables this to occur. To incorporate application well is hard work. Miller points out, "There is no harder work than change." Then he notes, "That is why the number one reaction to change is resistance." John Kotter, who teaches at the Harvard Business School, notes, "People change what they do less because they are given analysis that shifts their thinking than because they are shown a truth that influences their feelings."[240]

Kotter adds that the leader (preacher) must increase the sense of urgency so that the listeners cry out, "We must do something." That sounds like the crowd at the first Pentecost sermon. Kotter goes on to say that if we increase the sense of urgency, it will overcome or at least reduce complacency, fear, anger, and the pessimistic attitude that so often prevents change. This reinforces Broadus's contention that "application in the sermon is not merely an appendage to the discussion or a subordinate part of it, but is the main thing to be done.[241]

It would be a wonderful day in Christian pews and pulpits if everyone embraced the sentiments expressed by Norman Neaves:

> I'm tired of sermons that do not live where people live, that don't connect with the real stories and struggles by which their lives are shaped, that never touch earth or breathe the air the congregation breathes. Maybe there are

---

240 Miller, *Preaching*, 82; John F. Kotter and Dan S. Cohen, *The Heart of Change* (Boston: HBS Press, 2002), 1.

241 Ibid., v,17; Broadus, 210.

those who enjoy developing the universal sermon, the one
that can be preached everywhere and anywhere, that has
a quality of being timeless. But as far as I am concerned,
everywhere and anywhere mean nowhere; and those who
strive to be timeless, are usually, simply not very timely.

Great sermons incorporate strong application that creates a sense of urgency leading to change. [242]

Perhaps we need to be reminded that God's Word always demands a response. Did not James write, "But prove yourselves doers of the word, and not merely hearers who delude themselves"? When working to identify and express the text's application, look at the people you will be preaching to and ask, "What are the needs of these people, specifically?" Recall the first two questions I ask before I speak to any group. Who am I speaking to and what are their needs? From the perspective of their needs and in light of this text, what do these people need to know, feel, and do? Answering this question will be the key to identifying the application. [243]

Chapell draws our attention to the value of application when he writes, "Recognize that the chief purpose of application is not simply to give people something to do. Application gives ultimate meaning to the exposition." He explains, "Until we apply a truth, understanding of it remains incomplete. This means that until a preacher provides application, exposition remains incomplete."[244]

So, what can the preacher do to most effectively incorporate application? I suggest that it comes as you both exegete your text and exegete your people. Where these two intersect, you find fertile ground for application. As you undertake the former, ask, "What was this text intended to change in the lives of those who first heard it?" Put yourself in the place of those who first heard this portion of the Word. Look at the imperative verbs, the commands. Were these for that specific time and place, or are they universal in application? If appropriated, what changes are accomplished by obedience to these truths?[245]

Next, we need to examine what might limit the application of a particular text. The context? A complimentary text? Any cultural or unique historical conditions? Ask, is there anything in this passage that might lead

---

242 Chapell, 237.
243 James 1:22 (NASB)
244 Chapell, 203.
245 See Fabarez, 39–43.

me to conclude that this imperative is not to be taken as an application for today?[246]

What factors then might confirm this passage can be application specific? Does it address issues of character or the nature of man? Does it say anything about God's created order? Is anything included here with respect to God's constant unchanging standards for humanity?[247]

As you consider the people to whom you preach, what might your listeners have in common with those who first heard this text? In what ways would they contrast? How well are your listeners incorporating the text's imperatives and examples?[248] Robinson points out that when the preacher is uncertain about a text's application, the safest approach is to ask, what does this say about God? And what does this tell me about man's sin? He suggests that God's character and man's depravity are always constants. He also cautions us not to give weight to a "possible implication" that would be assigned to a "necessary implication."[249]

As the preacher examines the text and his listeners and thinks through developing his application, he must ask a series of questions. First, do my listeners understand what this text says, means, and implies? Without understanding, there can be no application.

Next, do my listeners believe the truths I am preaching? They may fully understanding the truths and not believe. Faith is a matter of the will. It is a matter of surrender. It is a matter of trust. If the listener has understanding, the next issue is does he believe? Does he believe what the Bible says about God's expectations and Jesus's commands? Does he believe the warnings? Does he believe the promises? Any appropriation of the application is predicated on the assumption that one believes! And at this juncture, the preacher can take the persuasive approach, "You can trust Him! He is trustworthy!" Or he might provide an example of someone who trusted God and God came through. You are trying to facilitate confidence in God and His Word.

When we move from belief to behavior, we actually are addressing a spectrum of application issues. In fact, the application may be positive or negative, start doing or cease doing! It is more than behavior. It is our attitudes, aspirations, expectations, activities, and words as well as what we do. Application can dictate and influence any or all of these areas.

---

246 Ibid., 43–45.
247 Ibid., 46–47.
248 Ibid., 49–50.
249 Haddon Robinson, "The Heresy of Application," in Larson and Robinson, 308–09.

When we draw application out of a text, we should be cautious. Robinson warns of the side-street of "legalism" that occurs when we take a principle, give an application, and then elevate that application to principle status. In fact, he maintains that more heresy is preached in application than in exegesis. There is heresy, he notes, when good truth is applied in the wrong way.[250]

Beyond asking people to change behavior based upon the imperatives of Scripture, the preacher needs to exhort the listener to change now, or maybe say, "Here is the first thing you can do." At times, the preacher needs to tell his hearers, "You can do this" and remind them that God will never ask them to do something He will not empower them to do.

When Chapell breaks down the application task, he asks four questions: First, "What does God require of me?" Next, "Where does God require it of me?" Third, "Why must I do what He requires?" And fourth, "How can I do what He requires?"

In detailing the second question, he provides a set of categories that might be considered by the preacher.

Does this passage say anything about:
1. Building proper relationships?
2. Reconciling conflicts?
3. Handling difficult situations?
4. Overcoming weakness or sin?
5. Lack or improper use of resources?
6. Meeting challenges and using opportunities?
7. Taking responsibility?
8. Honoring God?
9. Concern for social or world problems?[251]

In developing appropriate applications, Chapell notes that the preacher must first prove that the principle or truth comes from the text. Next, he maintains that it is the preacher's responsibility to demonstrate that the textual situation and the contemporary situation are an honest parallel. Finally, it is the preacher's responsibility to articulate the truth from Scripture in such a way that it can be honestly applied.[252]

Chapell points out that it is always wise for the preacher to provide reasons why obedience to the text and its application are the best course of

---

250 Robinson, "Blending," 297.
251 Chapell, 217–18; A similar list can be found in Veerman, 288.
252 Chapell, 218.

action. But he warns, make sure you, the preacher, are motivated by grace, and not guilt or greed.[253]

And most important, we are to tell people, "Here is how you do this. These are the steps." And again, we must encourage our listeners, "You can do this!" We must remind them that God will not require them to do anything He will not empower them to do. Moreover, God often demonstrates the benefits of obedience. Recall the phrase repeated in Matthew 6, "And your Father who sees in secret will reward you openly."[254]

Conclusion

Having worked our way through a study of application, permit me to provide for you a set of guidelines to work from as you endeavor to cultivate solid application in your sermons.

1. In your sermon, work at identifying appropriate applications. This will take time and effort.
2. Know that any solid application will connect the truth of what was said from the text to the life and experiences of the listeners.
3. Remember that application is always a summons to change. It may entail changing our minds, attitudes, behaviors, aspirations, or expectations. The goal is conformity of our lives to Christ.
4. Application should be given with passion and with a view to persuasion. Do not deal with life and death matters in a take it or leave it fashion.
5. Do not forget that application will address the mind, the emotions, and the will.

---

253 Ibid., 219
254 Ibid., 220–21; Matthew 6:1–2, 4–6, 18.

Chapter 15

The Beginning and the End

The preacher has one opportunity to make a first impression. Likewise, he will have one final moment to drive home his message. This being true, both deserve serious attention.

I have reserved discussion of the sermon's introduction and conclusion for the latter part of this volume because these two components of the sermon, in fact, should be the last portions to be written. Now that the preacher knows what he is saying in the body of the message, the introduction and conclusion can be tailor-made to fit exactly the content of the sermon's body. In this chapter, we will address four distinct issues and in this order: the title, the introduction, the conclusion, and the invitation.

The Title

Although not a lot of thought is given by many preachers, it is wise to expend some energy in crafting an appropriate title. The title is similar to the cover of a book or the label of a product. People often judge by appearance and make choices based upon first impressions, and the title of a sermon can at times help determine if someone will even come to hear the message. Of course, this is predicated particularly on whether the preacher or the church does any marketing. Many wise preachers will promote the sermon title on a marquee, on a website, in brochures, and in promotional material. The concept of putting many "hooks" in the water to attract prospective listeners is a wise step in the right direction.

I agree with Rick Warren that great titles are an art. In fact, if the preacher has talented people on his staff or in the church who work in the field of marketing, it is a good idea to ask for help. The point of the title is to attract and capture people's attention. And in this case, a team approach can be a wise decision.[255]

Warren points out that a good title will answer four questions. First, will it capture people's attention? Second, is it clear? Third, how appealing is it? And fourth, is it relevant? If you can get your titles to line up affirmatively with these questions, you have a winner. Warren does make one observation that I believe is important. In response to those who want to discount the importance of titles, he says, "Using sermon titles that appeal to felt needs isn't being shallow; it's being strategic." [256]

Here is one rule of thumb. Limit the number of words in your title to a maximum of eight. Any more and it can become both wordy and confusing.

The Introduction

The purpose of an introduction is to introduce the message. This almost goes without saying. I have heard discussions that the introduction should be extremely brief all the way up to the observation that it should constitute 20 percent or more of the sermon's length. A dissertation I read at Midwestern Seminary pointed out that John MacArthur's introductions average being 24 percent of his message. In the words of Spurgeon, that's a large front porch. Yet, the fact is, the introduction should accomplish its purpose, whether brief or extended.

Warren Wiersbe, one of my favorite preachers and writers, points out that introductions should be personal. He prefers shorter introductions and remarks. "If you take too long aiming your rifle, the game may disappear." He points out that the introduction's purpose is to declare the text and tell people why they should listen. In another discussion, he suggests three specific goals for the introduction. First, it serves to obtain the listener's attention. Second, it communicates the subject matter of the message. And third, it should convince the listener of the benefits of listening.[257]

Spurgeon advises his preachers, "As a rule do not make the introduction too long." He continues, "The introduction should have something sturdy

---

255 Rick Warren, "The Purpose-Driven Title" in Larson and Robinson, 371.
256 Ibid., 371–72.
257 Wiersbe, *Preaching*, 216–17; Ben Awbrey, *How Effective Sermons Begin* (Ross-shire: Mentor, 2008), 83.

in it. It is well to fire a starting shot as the signal gun to clear the decks for action."[258]

Broadus points out that the theme of the sermon should be communicated in the introduction or at least early in the message. He writes, "But usually the reader, or hearer, is more interested if in the introductions or early in the sermon there is a revealing statement of the heart of the message." Broadus points out later in his classic, "Even if your subject needs no introduction, your audience does." [259]

In Michael Hostetler's excellent volume, *Introducing the Sermon: The Art of Compelling Beginnings*, he points out, "If the introduction falters, the exposition may never be heard." He points out the incredible importance of capturing the audience's attention at the outset of the message. In order to do introductions well, he suggests a four-step approach where the preacher begins with the "secular" to build a bridge, announces the "biblical" to communicate his text, addresses the "personal" in order to communicate how the message will connect and benefit the hearer, and concludes with a "bridge" into the body of the message.[260]

Talbot Seminary's Kent Edwards writes an insightful essay on the sermon's introduction entitled, "Why Should I Listen to You?" He points out, as have many others, that the preacher has about three minutes to make a first impression and catch an audience's attention. He maintains that these first few minutes determine whether they will listen or check out mentally. Their bodies will be with you, but their minds and imagination will be somewhere else. He points out that the introduction will answer the question, "Why should I listen to you?"[261]

Edwards suggests that a good introduction succeeds if two objectives are met: they relate the audience to the speaker and the message's main idea. In his essay, he provides seven guidelines for crafting good introductions:

1. He encourages the preacher to begin with a "clear understanding of the idea of the sermon." Know what you want to say before you say it.
2. Develop interest by helping the listeners understand why it is in their best interest to listen.

---

258 Spurgeon, *Lectures*, 133.
259 Broadus, 56, 101.
260 Michael J. Hostetler, *Introducing the Sermon: The Art of Compelling Beginnings* (Grand Rapids: Zondervan Publishing House, 1986), 12–20.
261 Kent Edwards, "Why Should I Listen to You?" in Larson and Robinson, 372.

3. Write well so that the wording will be "striking, specific, and direct."

4. He encourages the preacher to "match the introduction to the mood of the sermon." He explains, "Effective preachers ensure that the emotions evoked by the introduction contribute to the overall mood of the message."

5. Adapt the introduction to "fit the structure of the sermon." If it is deductive, you begin with your conclusion and then argue the reasons why. If it is inductive, you examine the text and then ask, "What is God saying? What can we learn? Let's see."

6. He emphasizes the importance of delivery, suggesting that it needs authenticity, variety, and energy. He points out that the audience should sense that the speaker is in control.

7. Finally, he maintains that the preacher should be himself. [262]

John Stott also has some thoughts to contribute on the priority of the introduction. Like many other preachers, he maintains the importance of preparing the introduction and the conclusion after the body of the sermon has been prepared. He is a bit ambiguous when he contends that the introduction should be neither too short nor too long, but he does affirm solidly that the purpose of the introduction is to arouse interest and introduce the theme. In discussing the types of introductions, he maintains that the preacher can either take the traditional approach of announcing the text, or he can take the "situational" approach in an endeavor to start where people are.[263]

Another prominent preacher who has written on "Introducing the Sermon" is the former US Senate Chaplain, Lloyd John Ogilvie. Like Edwards, he points out that the preacher has about three minutes to "set the hook." Like many other preachers, he prepares his introduction after the message is complete. [264]

He emphasizes the importance of establishing the purpose of the message in the introduction. He encourages the preacher to take to heart the advice and example of Leslie Weatherhead, who for years served as the Senior Pastor of the City Temple in London. Weatherhead wrote:

> It is my practice, when I am trying to make a sermon, to write out at the head of a sheet of paper the aim of the sermon—what I hope the sermon will achieve. It is a good

---

262 Ibid., 373–74.
263 Stott, 244–45.
264 Lloyd John Ogilvie, "Introducing the Sermon" in Duduit, 176.

> thing for a preacher to keep that in mind lest he preach a
> sermon of interest, and perhaps, usefulness to himself, but
> to very few others. Let him set down in black and white
> what he expects his discourse will do.

Ogilvie maintains, "Without that kind of clarity and purpose, the sermon will aim at nothing and hit it" every time. Ogilvie's goal in his introduction, then, is "to state the purpose of the message in the most effective and varied form."[265]

Describing the content of the introduction, Ogilvie gives these four essentials. First, it should bring clarity to the message's purpose. This is what I am speaking about and why it is important. Second, the introduction should create empathy between the preacher and his listeners. They need to know that he understands them and cares about them. Third, the preacher needs to communicate the benefits or "takeaways" if the listener pays attention to the message. And fourth, he emphasizes the need for the preacher to use variety in his approaches to his introduction. He points out that predictability is the "preacher's bane and the congregation's boredom." [266]

In his essay, Ogilvie gives ten different types of introductions and suggests that the preacher use a different one each week so that he will minimize predictability, maximize variety, and capitalize on the congregation's openness to the introduction. Consider, then, his top ten approaches for injecting variety into the sermon's introduction.[267]

One, share a personal story from your own spiritual pilgrimage and then follow it up with the application of the text and the sermon's purpose statement.

Two, share a real-life human-interest story that gets to the heart of what you are preaching and then follow it up with the purpose and text.

Three, use an anecdote or parable from history or the contemporary scene that isolates the core issue of the text. Then press on with the purpose, text, and message.

Four, use a direct statement of the text and identify its promise for present-day life.

Five, make a sympathetic reference to some need well known in the audience and how the text offers the means for meeting that need.

Six, dramatically retell a Bible story from a first-person perspective. Then state the purpose and proceed with its relevance for the present.

---

265 Ibid., 176–77.
266 Ibid., 177.
267 Ibid.

Seven, make a straightforward declaration about a contemporary problem and then move to Scripture pointing out that God has a solution from His Word.

Eight, ask questions that get to the heart of a human need. He explains, "these 'do you ever …' questions should be followed by an 'of course, we all do' kind of empathy, and then the statement of how God can meet the need and how this message will help explain what He is ready to do."

Nine, communicate a clearly articulated paragraph of the essential truth which the entire message will address. Then break it down into its key ideas and proceed.

Ten, review a current news item that is on everyone's mind and focus in on God's Word for that situation. This provides an opportunity to demonstrate the relevance of God's Word for the contemporary scene. Moreover, it shows how God can meet our deepest needs.[268]

Each of these can be used to build a bridge into the preacher's message. He points out that, in each type of introduction, "there must be a note of urgency, authority, and vulnerability." The audience must understand that what they are hearing is crucial both for this time and eternity.[269]

In light, of these insights, what can we say by way of summary considering the critical importance of the introduction?

One, if you preach to the same audience on a weekly basis, work to vary the approaches to your introductions.

Two, I want to encourage you, at least in the first five years of your preaching ministry, to write out your introduction verbatim, memorize it (if not word for word, at least thought for thought), and deliver it, making full eye contact with your audience.

Three, prepare your introduction after the body of your message is complete. Then, you will know exactly what you are introducing.

Four, make sure that your introduction 1) establishes rapport with your audience; 2) creates interest in the subject; 3) clearly articulates the subject matter of the message; 4) explains the benefits for the listener if he grasps what you are saying; 5) introduces the text at hand; and 6) bridges into the body of the message.

You only have one opportunity to make a good first impression, so let me encourage you to be diligent in the preparation of your introduction![270]

---

268 Ibid., 177–78.

269 Ibid.

270 A good summary of the introduction can be found in Richard L. Mayhue, "Introductions, Illustrations, and Conclusions," in MacArthur, 242–47.

The Conclusion

From my perspective, the conclusion is the most important part of the sermon. It is the point of the sermon where everything is on the line. In biblical terms, it is the valley of decision. Broadus points out, "Preachers seldom neglect to prepare some introduction to a sermon but very often neglect the conclusion; and yet the latter is even more important than the former." Citing the great Greek and Roman orators on the conclusion (peroration), Broadus states, they "paid much attention to their preparation, seeming to feel that this was the final struggle which must decide the conflict and gathering up all their powers for one supreme effort." Broadus wisely insists that the preacher give the same thorough preparation to his conclusion.[271]

In the concluding moments, the issues addressed in the message have been clearly made, the application has been pressed, and decisions are now in the hands of the listener. Will the listener surrender? Will he change his thoughts, attitudes, aspirations, expectations, or behavior? "What will you do?" is the question in the conclusion. It is the point where the preacher must drive home his theme.

Stott again offers great insight. He points out that some preachers are incapable of ending anything, especially their sermons. Some are like planes that circle incessantly but cannot land due to fog. Stott calls this the "tragedy of aimlessness." He points out that other sermons in contrast end too abruptly, like a theatrical production without a finale or a music piece with no crescendo or climax. The conclusion deserves better than that![272]

He notes that the conclusion should not simply be a recapitulation of the main idea. "Truth," he maintains, "must be driven home by the hammer blows of repetition." Yet, "a good conclusion," says Stott, "drives past recapitulation to personal application." Although application should be made throughout the message, the conclusion is the moment where the preacher should make his final appeal with all the passion he can muster. Stott cites Cicero, who wrote, "An eloquent man must so speak as to teach, please, and persuade." It is this final element that must be the essence of the conclusion. As we wrote earlier, Augustine picked up on Cicero's admonitions and stated in his great work, *On Christian Doctrine*, that it is the responsibility of the preacher to "teach the mind, delight or inspire the

---

271 Broadus, 122–24.
272 Stott, 245–46.

affections (emotions), and move the will." "For," he continued, "to teach is a necessity, to please is sweetness, [and] to persuade is victory." [273]

Citing Broadus, Stott declares, "Our expectation, then, as the sermon comes to an end, is not merely that people will understand or remember or enjoy our teaching, but that they will do something about it. If there is no summons, there is no sermon."[274]

Stott continues to marshal the great preachers of history. He points out that the Puritans were known for finishing each sermon with the "use" or "application" to the conversion of souls and their training in holiness.[275]

He draws attention to G. Campbell Morgan, who wrote:

> The preacher is not merely asking a congregation to discuss a situation, and consider a proposition, or give attention to a theory. We are to storm the citadel of the will, and capture it for Jesus Christ ... Whether evangelizing or teaching does not matter. The appeal is the final thing.[276]

Next, Stott draws R. W. Dale to his witness stand. Dale asserts, "If we are to be successful, there must be vigorous intellectual activity, but it must be directed by a definite intention to produce a definite result." Citing Archbishop Whately, Dale said of some preachers, "He aimed at nothing, and hit it!" And from John Wilkins we are reminded, "The chief end of an orator (a preacher) is to persuade!"[277]

As the preacher moves to the conclusion, it is good to keep in mind the counsel of Richard Bernard, who wrote in 1607 that the goal of our preaching, our application, and our conclusion is to:

> Inform the ignorant, confirm such as have understanding, reclaim the vicious, encourage the virtuous, convince the erroneous, strengthen the weak, recover again the backslider, resolve those who have doubts, feed with milk and strong meat continually, in season and out of season.[278]

Brian Harbour quotes Andrew Blackwood concerning the importance of concluding well: "Apart from the text, the most vital part of the sermon is the conclusion." Harbour explains, "Being the last part of the sermon the

---

273 Ibid., 246.
274 Ibid.; Broadus, 210.
275 Stott, 247
276 Ibid., 247–48.
277 Ibid., 249.
278 Ibid., 252

listener will hear, the conclusion needs to summarize, restate, illustrate, or apply the sermon in such a way that the listener can take home the essence of the message." He concludes, "Effective preaching demands an effective ending."[279]

This and much more has been written about the importance of the conclusion for the sermon. Consider now some practical advice on how to prepare effective conclusions. From my perspective, an effective conclusion will transition into a time of invitation where people are invited to respond publicly to what they have heard. We will treat the invitation separately. Now, what are some principles for formulating and delivering an effective conclusion?

Here is some advice as you prepare your conclusion.

1. Let your conclusion reflect the sermon's main point or points.
2. Be clear and specific.
3. Focus on the text's application and demands.
4. Rely heavily on "will you …"
5. Stress in the conclusion that God wants, empowers, and expects the listener to change.
6. Know that the change may be in attitudes, aspirations, expectations, words, or behavior.
7. Communicate that it is just as important to stop some things as it is to start others.
8. Do not be afraid to use a stirring illustration to demonstrate the change you are demanding.
9. Be passionate in your appeal.
10. Do not consider trying to preview an upcoming sermon. That will only break the flow of thought.
11. Be sure to reserve enough energy so that you are not exhausted as you move into the conclusion.
12. Preach for a verdict.

Note that every sermon should be preached with the intention of seeing lives changed through the power of the Gospel. Each sermon should be preached for a verdict, or it should not be preached at all.

The Invitation

As I draw my conclusion to a close, I transition into the invitation. I am well aware that not everyone extends an invitation, but I do. I know

---

279 Brian Harbour, "Concluding the Sermon" in Duduit, 216.

that not everyone believes in the validity of an invitation, but I do. I have read Martyn Lloyd-Jones' critique of the invitation and simply believe he is wrong, both historically and theologically in this area. I do, however, have great respect for him in most other areas. When I extend an invitation, I am not equating that activity with one's salvation experience.[280]

When I extend an invitation, I am doing it as the pastor of a church. I am actually asking people if they will respond to what they have heard in the message. Seldom will I preach a message when I do not give a gospel invitation. I ask the congregation to bow their heads and close their eyes. I know that Christians will be praying and those who are not Christians will be listening.

Because I believe that the preaching of the Word of God is sacramental in its essence, that God extends grace through the preaching of His Word, I am confident that the Holy Spirit is active in His role to convict people of the reality of sin, righteousness, and judgment (John 16:8). I believe and expect, by faith, that the Lord will save the lost if they are willing to be saved. I do believe it is a matter of faith on the part of those who hear. I often quote John 1:12, "As many as received Him, to them He gave the right to become the children of God, even to those who believe in His name." Often I will quote Romans 10:13, "For whoever will call on the name of the Lord will be saved." My assumption is that those who "receive" and "call" are the elect.

Often I will say, "You are not here by mistake or accident. The Lord brought you here today. I want to ask you, if you have never invited Christ to come into your life, would you do that right now?" Then I might ask, "Is there any reason you cannot receive Jesus Christ right now?" Then I point out that what is important is not so much the words they say as the attitude of their heart. Then I ask, "Would you invite Christ to come into your life right now and save you?" Then I say to them, "Permit me to lead you in a salvation prayer ... if this expresses the desire of your heart." My assumption is that if they see their need and see God's free offer of salvation by His grace through their faith, they will pray. Many have!

Here is the prayer I usually use. I ask them to pray this to God after me:

---

280 D. Martyn Lloyd-Jones, *Preaching and Preachers* (Grand Rapids: Zondervan, 1971), 265–82. A sound response to Lloyd-Jones can be found in R. Alan Street, *The Effective Invitation* (Grand Rapids: Kregel Academics, 1984, 2004), 131–38.

> Dear God, I have sinned against You
> And I have lived selfishly
> And right now, I choose to turn away
> From my sin and my selfishness
> And I turn to You.
> I ask You to forgive me, clean me up on the inside,
> and make me brand new. Jesus,
> thank You for dying on the cross for me.
> Thank You for being raised from the dead for me.
> From this moment forward, I will,
> By faith, live for You. And some day, when this life is
> over,
> I will come home to Heaven and live with
> You forever.
> Jesus, I pray this in Your name, Amen.

Before you criticize this as an *"ex opere operato"* mindset, understand that it involves repentance, faith, and looking to Christ alone for salvation. Do you think that Christ would turn any away who prayed this in honesty and humility? I don't.

When the "amen" is said, I tell the congregation:

> I want to give you an opportunity to respond to what you
> have heard and done today. Some of you prayed to invite
> Christ into your heart and life for the very first time.
> Others of you would like to talk with someone about this.
> Some of you are believers who are away from God, and
> like the prodigal son, you know you need to come home
> and get right with your Heavenly Father. It may well be
> that some of you have unfinished business with God. So,
> as we stand, I am going to invite you to come. Some of you
> may have been visiting our church. You are a believer and
> you believe the Lord wants this to be your church home.
> For each of you, I invite you to come.

When people respond publicly to the invitation at the churches I have pastored, we always have them meet one on one with a decision counselor. We work with them to identify what spiritual need they are dealing with. As Christ's ambassador, it is especially the privilege of the preacher to encourage hearers to be reconciled to Christ (2 Cor. 5:20).

As you can tell, I believe it is imperative to be prayed up as well as studied up before you preach. I also believe it is of utmost importance to give time, energy, prayer, and thought to preparing your title, introduction, conclusion, and invitation.

Chapter 16

Preparation and Presentation

In our seminary orientation, I tell all the new students that if they master every subject but fail in their ability to communicate, they will be a failure in ministry. The New York Yankees have paid Mariano Rivera millions of dollars because he does something better than anyone else. He delivers a baseball, finishes games, and wins most of the time. In the end, preaching is like baseball; the delivery is of utmost importance. The pitch, the presentation, the delivery—these are critical. And success or failure in preaching is often dependent on both the preparation and the presentation.

When we think about biblical preaching, we think first of preparation; preparation of the messenger and then the message. Next, we think about the presentation; how the message is delivered. A sermon is not a sermon until it is preached. And when we preach, people should sense that the truth we share matters to us.

Perhaps you recall that Ben Franklin was a great admirer of the preaching of evangelist George Whitefield. Since he was not a professing Christian (he had a Quaker background but was more closely aligned with the Deists), someone asked Franklin why he went to hear the great evangelist. The point, related Franklin, was not that he believed Whitefield's words but that Whitefield believed them. I hope those who are not professing believers will think the same of us. They may not yet believe what we say, but we certainly do! People should sense that the Gospel, indeed, matters to us.[281]

---

281 Joel Gregory, "The Voice in Preaching," in Duduit, 396.

In order for us to move others, we must be moved ourselves. Howard Hendricks says insightfully, "The more thoroughly I know a concept, the more deeply I feel it, and the more consistently I practice it, the greater my potential as a communicator."[282]

Walter Kaizer, one of the preeminent Old Testament scholars of the past generation, wrote this:

> From the beginning of the sermon to its end, the all engrossing force of the text and the God who speaks through the text must dominate our whole being. With the burning power of truth on our heart and lips, every thought, emotion , and act of the will must be so captured by the truth that it springs forth with excitement, joy, sincerity, and reality as an evident token that God's Spirit is in that Word. Away with all mediocre, lifeless, boring, and lackluster orations offered as pitiful substitutes for the powerful Word of the living Lord.[283]

We need to be reminded of MacArthur's words, that "a good sermon poorly preached is no better than a poor sermon properly preached." He maintains, "One has light with no heat; the other has heat with no light." And both are substandard. Sadly, he tells us, "Worthwhile substance can be ineffective if communicated in an unskilled fashion." He concludes, "Every man who enters the pulpit must be conscious that his delivery will either enhance the exposition or detract from it."[284]

It is well to be reminded, moreover, of John Maxwell's observation. He writes, "Words are the currency of ideas and have the power to change the world." If that is the case, and it is, then every preacher should aspire to be one who "has something to say, and ... say it well." [285]

Presentation

Before we dig into the fundamental principles of delivery, I want to address a few issues related to the setting and presentation of the message.

Many congregations use video clips, dramas, and testimonies. The key is using these appropriately so that the message is enhanced. The primary

---

282 Howard G Hendricks, *Teaching To Change Lives* (Portland: Multnomah Press, 1987), 87.

283 John MacArthur, "Delivering the Exposition," in MacArthur, 326.

284 Ibid., 321, 324.

285 Maxwell, 67; York and Decker, 195.

use for a drama especially is to set up the issue at hand. What problem, dilemma, or spiritual issue are we dealing with? As a rule, the drama should clarify the problem, not offer solutions. That is the role of the sermon.

Video clips can be used like a drama, or they can be used to illustrate a main point. Be cautious not to allow the video clip to overshadow the biblical message. Make doubly sure that it illustrates accurately what you want clarified from the message.

Testimonies can be used at the beginning, middle, or conclusion of the message. At the beginning, it can highlight the subject that will be addressed. In the middle, it can either verify what has been said, or it can be used to confirm what has been said. At the end of the message, it can be used especially to verify the significance and the truthfulness of what has been said and point people to the Lord as the ultimate answer to life's most critical problem.

Several years ago, I preached a pro-life message on a pro-life Sunday emphasis. Before I preached, I introduced Gianna Jessen, a fascinating young lady who had Cerebral Palsy. She had been aborted as an infant with a saline abortion but had refused to die. She shared her story for the millions of babies who did not survive that horrific procedure. By the time I stood to preach, everyone was eager to hear God's perspective.

If you use video clips, dramas, or testimonies, make sure that they enhance the message and are not a detraction. It is better not to use these than to use them poorly.

Another issue that has been important for me is the whole notion of the pulpit. Some call this a "sacred desk." Eventually I transitioned from a large pulpit to an open pulpit, to an acrylic (you almost can't tell it is there) pulpit, to no pulpit. I discovered over the years that the pulpit was actually a psychological barrier. The last ten years of being a senior pastor, I simply did away with it. I did use a small table (about a foot square) to periodically lay my Bible on. My major preoccupation was not to have any barriers between myself and the congregation. If you have a pulpit, then when you preach, I advise you to get out from behind it as quickly as possible and preach with your whole body.

In the service, I encourage you to pay particular attention to the light, sound, staging, and temperature. All of these issues should be conducive to an uninterrupted worship experience.

Let me remind you again that if by chance you are preaching in a large worship center with cameras and a big screen, you should be aware that after the fifth row back from the front, most people will be watching the screen. If you want to talk directly to them, look into the camera. They will feel as though you are talking directly to them.

In the service and with the sermon, it was my custom to insert interactive outlines in the bulletin. They were usually an 8 ½ x 11" sheet of paper with a center fold. I would include the outline of my message and salient points from the message. I would, however, leave key words blank so that the listeners could fill them in as the message unfolded. It did take working ahead to make this happen. As I have said before, for type A personalities, like myself, I would always put the answers to the blanks at the bottom of the last page. If not, I would find myself bombarded after the service. "What was number three?" The reason I did this was so that people could take home what they had heard. I recall what my Uncle Ralph said (again), "The palest ink is stronger than the strongest mind." I wanted our people to learn what Scripture had to say.

One other "presentation" issue has to do with getting feedback. These are of two sorts, "immediate" and "ultimate." Often when I was preaching, I would ask the congregation to respond or say something with me. This was for the purpose of engaging them. For example, a few months ago I did a series on the church from Ephesians. I had everyone raise their right hand and point their finger up and say, "I am," and then point to themselves and say, "the church." It was to help reinforce the idea that the church is people and not a physical building or a location.

Nonetheless, as you preach, watch the congregation to make sure they are engaged with you. It is usually not difficult to tell. And your goal is to have them with you as you preach.

Another type of feedback was after the service. I wanted to know if anything did not connect. I suggest you get this from a trusted staff member or leader in the church who has your best interest at heart or even your spouse. Your goal is to get better, not get a pat on the back. For some reason, when folks would say, "Great sermon," I just let it roll off like water off a duck's back. Actually, I wanted to ask, "What did you like about it?" But I knew we did not have time for that discussion, and their comment may have just been their way of being nice.

Delivery

When we discuss the subject of delivery, there are actually two components that need to be addressed. The first is how you say, and the second is what you do. And both are critically important. Consider first how you say what you say.

I challenge you to work at how you speak. Work at maintaining good vocal health to begin with. This means getting sufficient rest, avoiding yelling, and drinking plenty of liquids. Avoid straining to clear your throat because this can irritate your vocal cords. Some advise preachers to avoid using throat lozenges because they can dry out the throat. It is probably a good idea to avoid loud environments. Trying to communicate here can put a strain on both the ears and the voice.[286] In short, take care of your voice.

When preaching, make sure you use full vocal production where you push with the diaphragm. Work at breathing deeply. Let your pitch be natural. One voice coach suggested that the speaker, or preacher, find the lowest note on a piano that he can sing, go up a third of an octave, and concluded that that pitch will be the center of a preacher's normal pitch range. Joel Gregory points out that when a speaker gets nervous or agitated, the tightening of the throat can cause the pitch to rise as the sermon continues. Work to relax the throat. [287]

With respect to the pace or the rate of the sermon, Gregory had this wise counsel:

> It is my opinion that when you come to the application of preaching—when you are making an assault on the will of people to change the parliament of their personality—that needs to be the fastest pace. It is as if you are firing shots, trying to lay siege to their will—explaining at a slow rate, illustrating at a mid rate, seeking to change behavior at a fast rate.[288]

All good preaching utilizes variety in both pitch and pace.

An additional component of good vocal production is volume. All good speakers know to use a variation. Being loud or soft can help the preacher communicate. Sometimes the greatest intensity is communicated in a very soft voice. Varying pitch, rate, and volume can help the preacher communicate effectively.

Coupled with this is my advice to be expressive. Let the bold statements be bold! Let the intense statements be intense!

Work at clearly articulating and enunciating your words. Depending on what part of the country or world you are from, you will no doubt be

---

286 Emily Shive, "No Voice, No Preach" in Larson and Robinson, 611.
287 Gregory, 394–95.
288 Ibid., 394.

partial to local dialects. If it is a distracting mannerism, you should work on this. I know that my preaching professor, Al Fasol, used to get on to us for using "gist, git, and fer" for "just, get, and for." If you are like me and were raised in the South, I have penchant for saying "thang" instead of "thing." These can be worked on. One of the best preaching students I ever had came from the coal mining district in the mountains of southwest Virginia. Mountain vernacular often had subject-verb disagreement like "he done …" He worked on this to correct it. He will be one of the great preachers of the up and coming generation. Other students drop the endings of some words like "preachin'" instead of "preaching." Again, these are the kinds of things the preacher can work on and should.

Something else you can do that will assist delivery of your message is to utilize the dramatic pause. Say something important, and then pause to let it sink in or think your next thought or both. Dramatic pauses give impact to our words. Maxwell calls this pausing strategically to "give your audience time to think about what you have said."[289]

Remember, it is through your voice and your words that you communicate not only information but also emotion. Even Augustine understood the great value of pathos (feeling or emotion). And it is well to be reminded that people listen for our emotions as much as our ideas. Citing Bruce Shelley, Jeffrey Arthurs contends, "Ordinary people listen for the preacher's feelings as much as his ideas, perhaps more. That is simply part of the power of the spoken word." Modern communication theorists argue, "Listeners grant attention only to what interests them, and what interests them is what they feel they need." All of that is communicated through the preacher's voice. It is interesting that York and Decker point out, "Salesmen have long known that people buy on emotion and justify with facts."[290]

The way the preacher speaks will dictate and display his sense of authority, intensity, urgency, sincerity, confidence, and passion. I teach my students that we are not self-confident but God confident. If God has called us to preach, gives us a platform, and gives us a message, we should be brave as lions. I teach my students, when you stand to preach, be bold. Act like you own the place. You represent the One who does.

I like the summary made by Maxwell: "Tone, timing, volume, pacing—everything you do with your voice communicates something

---

289 Maxwell, 71; See York & Decker, 248.
290 Jeffrey Arthurs, "Pathos Needed," in Larson and Robinson, 594; York and Decker, 210.

and has the potential to help you connect or disconnect from others when you speak."[291]

But the delivery is not just the way we speak; it is also what we do in the pulpit. When the preacher stands to preach, he should walk confidently to the center of the platform, however large or small. The preacher needs to display an air of confidence. He needs to make a good visual impression. He needs to be neat and well-dressed, whether it be casual or more formal. York and Decker comment that the preacher should present himself in such a way that does not detract from the message he wants his hearer to grasp. One rule of thumb is to dress one notch above what the average person in the congregation is wearing. I will let the reader use discretion here.[292]

I also want to encourage the preacher to display good posture. Stand up straight, square your shoulders, and act like you belong in the pulpit. It is important to display confidence and energy in our body position and movement. York and Decker cite Malcolm Forbes, who wrote, "Stand tall. The difference between towering and cowering is totally a matter of inner posture. It's got nothing to do with height, it costs nothing and it's more fun!"[293]

Something else we can do in the pulpit is work at utilizing effective and appropriate gestures. With gestures, be natural and relaxed. Use gestures as though you were talking to someone one on one and face to face. Be aware, however, that the larger the crowd, the more exaggerated your gestures will need to become.

Let me point out again that sometimes we learn by good examples and sometimes we learn by bad examples. I suggest to my students that they observe commercials by local car dealerships. Invariably the spokesman or spokeswoman uses awkward gestures. I point out that normally, they will show you how not to use gestures.

The next thing I remind my students to do is smile. Maxwell teaches that one of the most important things the speaker can do is smile. It helps the people present know that you are happy to be speaking to them and that you are glad and grateful to be there.[294]

Closely connected to smiling is the importance of making eye contact. To look people right in the eye says, "I care about you." The old notion of

---

291 Maxwell, 68.
292 York and Decker, 224.
293 Ibid., 224, 233.
294 Maxwell, 71

looking over people's heads is worthless. York and Decker share this from Ralph Waldo Emerson:

> An eye can threaten like a loaded and level gun; or can insult like hissing and kicking; or in its altered mood by beams of kindness, make the heart dance with joy.

Our goal is to look into the eyes of those to whom we speak with confidence.[295]

The next thing the preacher can do is to make a firm commitment to not be tied to his notes. I recommend that the preacher take as few notes as possible into the pulpit. I am not one who argues for "no notes." Take enough to stay aware of your message's flow. But do not let them hinder your ability to communicate. The more you have to look at your notes, the less you can look at your audience.

Display plenty of energy. The bottom line is we preach with our whole body. Be emphatic!

And last, work at overcoming any distracting mannerisms. There are two ways we can do this. First, ask someone or a few people you trust to give you feedback. "Am I saying or doing anything that is a distraction?" The preacher can also videotape himself preaching and do a self-critique. The camera does not lie.

Distracting mannerisms are legion. Some students are shocked at the number of "ums" or "ahs" I have counted. Others shuffle their feet, play with the change in their pocket, or keep touching their face. Others use filler phrases like, "You know." Actually, you can make your own list. The point is, we want to remove anything that may prove to be a distraction from the preaching of God's Word. Removing distracting mannerisms can be hard work, but it is well worth the effort. And the sooner you can deal with these, the more effective you will be as a communicator.

Each semester I warn my students against committing the cardinal sin of boring people. How we can take the greatest message in human history and make it boring just astounds me. But some do. As a result, I give them a checklist on what is required to bore people and use every persuasive bone in this professor's body to discourage its implementation. Here is my list of ten steps that guarantee boredom in the pew. If I knew where this came from, I would give credit, but I do not. Here is a checklist of what not to do.

---

295 York and Decker, 226.

1. Be sure to speak in a monotone voice. You dare not vary your rate, volume, or pitch.
2. Be sure to read your sermon material verbatim.
3. Better yet, be so unfamiliar with your material that your listeners are wondering what you are trying to accomplish.
4. Stand still. Do not move. Show no energy.
5. You dare not make eye contact. Someone might think you are speaking to them.
6. Since you do not have enough material, be sure to repeat yourself over and over again.
7. Get on one track or the other. Talk too fast or too slow; either will work just fine.
8. Do not dare to show any variety or say anything interesting.
9. You dare not show any enthusiasm, emotion, or passion.
10. Do not dare take your message seriously.

Permit me to conclude the chapter on presentation and delivery with some wise words from the great preacher G. Campbell Morgan, who explained that passion is an essential ingredient for effective delivery:

> In explaining what he means by "passion," he recalls a discussion the English actor Mccready had with a well-known pastor. The pastor was trying to understand why crowds flocked to the fictional plays but few came to hear him preach God's changeless truth. Mccready responded, "This is quite simple....I present my fiction as though it were truth, you present your truth as though it were fiction." [296]

Let me encourage you to work diligently at your presentation and delivery. Eternity is staked on those who proclaim it. We dare not give the Lord anything less than our absolute best!

---

[296] G. Campbell Morgan, *Preaching* (Grand Rapids: Baker Books, reprinted 1974), 36 in MacArthur, "Delivering" in MacArthur, 325.

Index

Scripture

Made in the USA
San Bernardino, CA
14 March 2014